LIVING
THE
SACRAMENTS
A CALL TO CONVERSION

LIVING THE SACRAMENTS

A CALL TO CONVERSION

Fr. David M. Knight

Our Sunday Visitor, Inc.
Huntington, Indiana 46750

Library of Congress Catalogue No: 85-60888
ISBN 0-87973-815-4

Printed in the United States of America

Table of Contents

PART FOUR

Matrimony and Holy Orders: The Sacraments of Community
Page 63

PART FIVE

Anointing and Eucharist: The Sacraments of Enduring Love
Page 91

The Plan of This Book

SACRAMENT	GIFT OF SPIRIT	FRUIT OF SPIRIT	A CALL AND COMMITMENT TO	CELEBRATED IN EUCHARIST IN
Baptism	Understanding	Joy	Relationship with Christ	Introductory Rites
Reconciliation	Knowledge	Faith	Discipleship and Prayer	Liturgy of the Word
Confirmation	Fear of Lord	Peace and Self Control	Witness and Mission	Presentation of Gifts
Matrimony and Holy Orders	Piety Counsel	Patience and Kindness Gentleness	Mediate Christ's Life in Community	Consecration and Elevation
Anointing and Eucharist	Fortitude Wisdom	Generosity Love	The Apostolate of Transforming the World	Communion Service

A Call To Conversion

An invitation to conscious interaction with God

An exciting change is taking place in the Church. The Church is changing from a maintenance goal to a growth goal. And the growth isn't growth in numbers; it is personal growth in the love and life of God.

To more and more people, being Catholic is coming to mean more than just "keeping in the state of grace." Forward motion is the name of the game. From now on, it will be increasingly difficult for any of us to consider ourselves Christians if we are not experiencing the life of grace as a dynamic process of conscious interaction with God.

A summons from the signs of the times

A frightening prospect? Or one that sounds too good to be true? However one answers that question, the fact is that today's situation calls for a *metanoia* — a change of mind from top to bottom of the Church. This is what the "signs of the times" are saying to the Church.

There is nothing surprising about the fact that a change of direction should be in the air. The Gospels begin with the proclamation, "Reform your lives! the reign of God has begun!" The constantly repeated Christian experience is that something new has happened which calls for a change of course. New attitudes, new values, new goals will characterize those who believe.

One "sign of the times" is the number of people defecting from the Church. Another is the drop in private confessions. Another is the fact that Sundays and holy days are not being observed as they used to be. And the saints are becoming strangers to their own people.

Catholics just aren't buying the religious practices which nourished their parents' devotion — or their own childhood faith. Like most signs of the times, this is both bad and good.

The good news — and the optimistic side of the picture — is that people are turning away from routine practices of religion because they recognize them to be shallow — or insufficient, or just not nourishing enough for their religious appetite. Something in the heart of Catholics is echoing the indictment of Isaiah 58: "Do you call this a fast. . . ?" (all these superficial observances): "This, rather, is the fasting that I wish: releasing those bound unjustly . . . setting free the oppressed . . . sharing your bread with the hungry . . . sheltering the oppressed and the homeless. . . ."

The same Catholics who find no meaning in the Mass or the sacraments, in Sunday sermons or Catholic education, in giving up something for Lent or taking on extra prayers, these same Catholics can vibrate to the call of the peace movement or give up wealth and social position to answer the cry of the afflicted. They are drawn to the healing professions, to special education and therapy for the handicapped. They work for the public defender's office and in programs to rehabilitate juvenile offenders, parolees and drug addicts. They volunteer for the Peace Corps and for other programs overseas and in Third World countries. They are generous; they are searching; and they are lost.

That is the bad news. They have found a noble direction but lost the true path. They have caught the spirit of Christ the Healer and at the same time abandoned Christ the Teacher — or at least the Christ who teaches in His Church. Away from the teaching of the Church — away from her doctrinal balance and the sustaining strength of her sacramental life; away from the nourishment of the Eucharist and the healing power of Reconciliation — they wander and weaken. Even while they swim to the rescue of others they are losing their own sense of where the shore is. Like so many actions of the young, theirs is gallantry and tragedy combined.

2

There is more bad news. Where the Catholicism they were brought up with fails to hold youths, the evangelical religions — and sometimes even the cults — are able to inspire them. One thinks of the Lord's complaint to Jeremiah: "Two evils have my people done: they have forsaken me, the source of living waters; they have dug for themselves cisterns, broken cisterns that hold no water."

What change of course is called for? This is not the time for conservatives and liberals to square off again about Vatican II. Nor is it the time to narrow focus down to some particular practice and to argue whether this policy or that is eroding the Faith. Something more general is called for.

The Church must convert from a religion of *maintenance* to a religion of *spiritual growth*.

Most Catholics grow up with the idea that holiness means keeping within bounds. To be holy means not to sin. Most parishes are geared to keeping people up to a par level of religious observance. Priests spend their time reconciling sinners, counseling members who have problems, fixing up bad marriages, and administering sacraments to people who may or may not understand the real meaning of the rituals or the sacraments' power and challenge in their lives.

In most parishes, if people were asked what "stage of development" their spiritual life was, they could only respond with blank, uncomprehending stares. To be a good Catholic means to keep the rules. It is a holding operation. What more can be expected, either of priests or of the parishioners, than just to keep the Catholic thing going? This means to get the kids through First Communion, Confirmation and (with a little luck) a marriage in the Church; and to keep going to Mass and Communion every Sunday. Catholicism is lived as a pattern of life; it is not something anybody thinks of as a way of growth.

This has got to change. There are signs that the change is beginning. The Church is facing a challenge as serious as that of the Protestant Reformation. The problem is not doctrine; it wasn't then and it isn't now. The problem is in the area of *spirituality*. The challenge for all Catholics is to *live out* Catholic belief in a way that enhances their lives. The challenge for those in ministry is to provide a pastoral care which fosters growth in grace.

3

It is a fact of experience that people tend to accept any doctrine so long as it is preached enthusiastically in a church which nourishes their spiritual life. The sophisticated college graduates who accept uncritically the "myths and fables" of new-found paganism, or the baseless evangelism of shallow fundamentalist preachers, are proof of this.

The working principle seems to be that whatever gives life — or even feels like it does — must be the way and the truth. So the "Bible churches" flourish — those enthusiastic, non-denominational communities with heart-stirring preaching, warm fellowship and supportive programs for family life which provide what the public wants — and has a right to!

It matters little to their members that these churches hang on the branches of Christianity like moss on a tree: without roots, tradition or theology. The over-simplification they indulge in is patent: the preachers of "instant religion" take what is most easily accessible in Christianity and make it even more accessible to people whose need is desperate. The relief they provide is superficial, but it is instantaneous and it is real.

Shallow as they are, these religious bubble-groups are providing people with a spiritual nourishment and an experience of enhanced life which they have never tasted in the established churches. This lends frightening confirmation to the hypothesis with which we began: that people will accept almost any way and any truth so long as they experience it as life.

The challenge to Catholicism is simply this: to translate her way, which is solid, and her truth, which is real, into life that can be experienced.

This calls for deeper prayer on the part of individuals; more growth-oriented ministry on the part of priests and parish teams; more expressive sharing of faith on all levels of the Christian community: families, support groups and parishes. It calls for a new sense of the Church's mission to transform the world.

When the whole Church — not just the parents, not just the priests and Religious, not just the youths, not just anybody except ourselves, but the whole Church, every single member of the People of God — accepts this challenge seriously, then there will be hope of new life.

4

This is the *metanoia*, the change of mind and of direction, to which the "signs of the times" are inviting the Church in this day entrusted to us.

The chapters which follow will show us how to respond to this invitation in two ways:

— by living the sacraments — all seven of them — seven days a week;

— by making friendship with Jesus Christ the most conscious experience of our lives.

This is an invitation to conscious interaction with God.

PART ONE

Baptism
And Relationship
With Christ

The call to be a Christian

CHAPTER 1

A Conversion To Relationship

*Living the Sacrament
of Baptism every day*

The Gospel is a call to conversion. This is less a conversion *from* something than a conversion *to* something. That "something" is *personal relationship* — friendship — with Jesus Christ.

This relationship is based on a choice. The choice, if it is fully and consciously made, is a choice to base the rest of one's life on interaction with Jesus Christ.

Baptism is the act which expresses that choice. It is called "the sacrament of faith," because it is our first sacramental expression of belief in Jesus Christ. Baptism is an *expression* of faith, and it empowers us to *experience* faith as a sharing in the divine knowledge of God.

An act of conscious choice

For most of us, baptism was not the moment when we chose relationship with Jesus — or chose anything else — on the conscious level at all. Most of us were baptized as babies. As we grew up, it is true, we ratified the choice that was made for us by our parents and sponsors. We accepted to be what we were. We accepted the gift of faith that had been given us and tried to walk by its light. We accepted the hope of eternal life that had become a part of us, and we embraced the promise of heaven as our destiny. We entered into the love of God that was poured out into our hearts with the gift of the Holy Spirit. We were grateful for His love and we pledged our love in return.

All this was a personal ratification of our baptism. It

9

was real; it was free; it was personal. It just may not have been as explicit and conscious as it should have been. That is why it is good for us to take a good clear look at baptism now — now that we are old enough to understand it, and mature enough in our faith to commit ourselves to it more deeply. To what does our baptism commit us? What does it give us? Have we made the commitment in its entirety? Are we making use of all that was given to us in baptism?

A relationship to live out daily

Being baptized is like being married: it isn't just something that happened to us once in our lifetime, perhaps many years ago. It is an ongoing, daily experience. It is not just that we *were* baptized; we *are* baptized. As for married people, the ceremony which put us into relationship with Christ was only the beginning. That ceremony pledged us to a lifetime of interaction which we experience every day.

One of the things we experience every day is the reality of what we are. A person who is blind experiences blindness every day; that is his reality. In the same way, people who are sighted experience seeing every day — or do they? Do some people take seeing so much for granted that they lose the experience of sight? Do they wind up seeing so much and noticing so little that they can hardly claim any experience of vision at all?

Baptism can be like that. Or baptism can be an experience of new life in relationship with Jesus Christ which we exult in every day.

Baptism is the gift of new life. We are called to live, and baptism has empowered us to live, on a level higher than the human. We should wake up every morning conscious that we are not only alive, but baptized into sharing in the life of God. As Christians we are able to do what only God can do, and we should experience ourselves doing this every day.

What is "higher" about the life and action of the baptized?

It is too simple to say that those who live in relationship with Christ are "more moral." They might be this, and certainly should be this, but not simply by the standards of decent people in society.

To the majority of educated, upright and self-respecting members of any society, the morality Christians are called upon to live could appear as just plain foolishness. We can expect this.

Jesus did not teach attitudes and values which are acceptable to any society or ethnic group on the basis of reason and culture alone. Jesus taught a morality (if the word itself does not fall short) based on the attitude of God himself. He taught us to be and to act exactly like God.

To do this we have to see things as God himself sees them. We have to "put on" the mind of God (see Matthew 5:48; 1 Corinthians 1:18; Philippians 2:5).

The Gifts of the Holy Spirit

People familiar with computers will recognize immediately that we have a problem here of "interfacing."

Two computers of different make can't always "talk" to each other. The communication system built into one may be so different from the system built into the other that they just can't receive signals from each other. They don't speak the same "language."

When this happens, some computer engineer designs an "interface card" — a device which, when inserted into one computer, will make it able to "hear" another.

That is what God did for us when He sent us the Holy Spirit.

God speaks a different language from us. Not only that, He doesn't even think the same way we do:

For my thoughts are not your thoughts,
nor are your ways my ways, says the LORD.
As high as the heavens are above the earth,
so high are my ways above your ways
and my thoughts above your thoughts.   (Isaiah 55:8-9)

God's answer to this situation was to bridge the gap: first by sending us Jesus Christ, who was God made human like us; then by sending us the Holy Spirit to dwell in our hearts.

The Holy Spirit's action within us has been studied under the names of seven "gifts of the Holy Spirit" (see Isaiah 2:2-3 and add Piety). These gifts are like interface cards: they enable our minds to interface with the mind of God, our wills to interface with His will. They enable us to receive the communication of His light, His power, His love.

The Gift of Understanding

Understanding is the Gift of the Holy Spirit most appropriate to think about in association with baptism. Understanding is the gift which enables us to "see" that the truths revealed by God are not only credible, but true.

By the Gift of Understanding we find it easy, even natural, to believe and to live by mysteries intelligible to God alone. This gift comes to us through baptism.

In the Greek Church baptism is sometimes just called "enlightenment." This puts the focus on baptism as the sacrament of faith and understanding, or the sacrament which gives us a share in the divine knowing of God.

Each one of us has particular experience of the Gift of Understanding. Ask yourself what truths of faith there are which you find so easy to believe that they seem almost evident to you. Do you find it easy to believe that Jesus is both man and God? That He really loves you individually as a person? That He is present in the Eucharist and given to you in love when you receive Communion? That there is life after death? That the Church on earth speaks and ministers with the power of Christ? That in sacramental confession you are encountering Jesus himself in the person of the priest?

To many people one or more of these truths constitute a real stumbling block to faith. Others believe them, but with so much confusion and struggle that they are hardly able to live by their belief.

Where you find it easy and natural to believe a mystery of the Faith, and where that mystery seems so clear to you in its meaning and significance for your life that you rejoice in living it, there you experience the Gift of Understanding. And in this gift you experience your baptism giving a new level — a divine level — to your life and knowing.

The Fruits of the Spirit — Joy

God is the fullness of life. The more we share in God's life, the more our own lives are enriched, our own being enhanced. As we surrender more and more to the Spirit who dwells within us, He is able to conform us more and more to Christ, to make us more and more like God in our thinking, choosing, loving and acting. This effect of the Spirit's action within us is called the "fruit of the Spirit." St. Paul gives us nine words to describe the effect of union with the Spirit of Christ. They are *love, joy, peace, patient endurance, kindness, generosity, faith, mildness* and *chastity* or self-control (see Galatians 5:22-23).

The "Fruit of the Spirit" which most naturally follows on understanding is *Joy*. In the measure that we grasp with our minds how real and true and meaningful the mystery of our salvation is, in the same measure we experience the joy of the Good News (see Romans 15:13; Ephesians 2:17-18; 3:14-18; 1 Thessalonians 1:6). Our baptism is a source of joy. It is, in fact, the source of all our joy, because through baptism we enter into life-giving relationship with God through Christ. "In Him" we become members of His Body, children of the Father, temples of His indwelling Spirit.

If, then, we find ourselves caught up in sadness, anxiety or depression, our first move should be toward the Gift of Understanding. The remedy to darkness is light. Through the Gift of Understanding the truth of our baptism — the grace of our salvation — becomes light and clarity to us.

The answer to sadness is the Good News. The Gift of the Holy Spirit which enables us to see this Good News in all of its reality is understanding. The fruit of this gift is joy.

Celebration of baptism in Eucharist

We celebrate the meaning of baptism in our lives during the Introductory Rite of the Mass.

The joy of the Good News is the fruit of *Evangelization*. And every celebration of the Eucharist begins with a "flashback" to the day of our own evangelization; that is, to the day when we ourselves first heard and believed the Good News. During the Introductory Rite (from the beginning of Mass to the Opening Prayer) we rejoice again in the relationship with God and with others which is ours through baptism: "May the grace of our Lord Jesus Christ, and the love of God and the fellowship of the Holy Spirit be with you all!"

In some eucharistic celebrations water is blessed at this point and sprinkled on the people as a reminder of baptism. If this ceremony is not used, there is instead the triple prayer: "Lord, have mercy; Christ, have mercy; Lord, have mercy." This is not just an act of begging pardon for sins.

In English the phrase "have mercy" evokes the image of a terrified sinner cringing under the upraised arm of God. Traced back to its Greek and Hebrew origins, however, the expression "have mercy" means "to come to the aid of another out of a sense of relationship."

Now we see why the prayer is repeated three times. We pray, "Lord have mercy"; "Christ have mercy"; "Lord have mercy" in an act of claiming the threefold relationship with God which is ours through baptism.

Jesus is Lord. We recall that He entered into His Lordship through His passion and death on the cross which we are about to celebrate in Eucharist. Because He is Lord He has been able to make us His Body through baptism. And now "in Christ" we enjoy relationship with Father, Son and Spirit. We claim this relationship — and the help that follows on it — as we give Jesus the titles of "Lord" and "Christ."

Through Jesus God has become our Father. "In Christ" we have become "sons in the Son." In Christ, we are redeemed and saved as members of His Body. From Jesus and the Father we have received the gift of the Holy Spirit, who is now our indwelling "Paraclete" — that is, Comforter, Helper and Guide.

We celebrate the fact, then, that Jesus came to reconcile us to the Father, to unite us to himself, and to send us the Holy Spirit. We call on Him to come to our aid because of the relationship we have with Him as children of the Father, members of His Body and temples of the Holy Spirit. We claim our relationship with God; and we claim the love and help of God which follow from it. In other words, we claim the consequence of our baptism. We claim the Good News.

Living our baptism

How do we, in practical terms, live out this relationship? The answer is by actively living out faith, hope and love. We live out faith by *expressing* faith in our actions, in our words, in

14

our choices. We live out hope by making choices based on the trust we have in God and His promises. We live out love by doing what is pleasing to God and helpful to our neighbor. We live all three by praying to God as our Father, following Jesus as our Savior, and listening for the inspirations of His Spirit in our hearts.

If, therefore, I notice that joy is diminished in my life, I can ask what truth of faith I am not being aware of with sufficient meaningfulness. I can then call on the Gift of Understanding and make a conscious act of faith in that truth (e.g. that I am a beloved child of God), asking for understanding. Then I can do something to *express* this act of faith (e.g., say an Our Father, start smiling). I can remember my baptism and rejoice again in the Good News.

If we choose to do so, we can make explicit now on a conscious, deep level our commitment to *relationship with Christ*. This relationship is already ours through baptism, but we need to begin *living* our baptism every day as an experience of relationship with God.

This is the most basic acceptance and experience of what it means to be a *Christian*.

CHAPTER 2

Do I Have a Friendship With Jesus?

*A choice
to interact*

Friends interact. How do I interact with the person of Jesus Christ?

By baptism we entered into a relationship with Jesus Christ — and this is a relationship of friendship. A real relationship, however — with anybody — is based on *interaction.* If I do not interact with Jesus Christ, how real is my relationship with Him? And if I do interact with Him, am I able to confidently "own" the fact that I am in relationship with Him as His friend?

It is the soul of Christian belief that Jesus rose from the dead to continue living and acting on earth in human form. He does this through His Church, His real and living Body on earth. In the Church, then, we should be able to encounter, to deal with, and to experience the presence of the risen, living Christ.

The Church is meant to be a milieu of living encounter with God.

If this is so, then our authentic experience of the Church will be measured by the "length and breadth and height and depth" of the experience of Jesus Christ which we have found through interacting with Him in the Church.

How does this interaction take place?

One way that friends interact is through words. Later we will speak about levels of communication with God in prayer. But the psychologists tell us that 80 percent of human communication is non-verbal. Words serve largely to explain, to make explicit, what we have already observed or expressed in non-verbal ways. The words of our religion serve us best when they articulate, when they make clear and explicit, what we have already *experienced* of Christ's action on us through the Church.

This action is constantly taking place. But to experience it we have to be in touch with our hearts.

Whether we are aware of it or not, whether we can pin-point the moments of its manifestation, every one of us is experiencing constantly the life and action of God within our hearts. Our experience of life is a mystical experience. The mystery of our being is a mystery of shared life with God through grace. The Holy Spirit is poured out in our hearts, active and alive. The goal of religious formation is to make us aware of this silent but eloquent self-expression of God in our lives — both within us and outside of us. Religious instruction should be faith experience brought to understanding.

Faith is the key

To say this is to say that faith is the foundation of all experience of Christ in the Church. To be aware of our relationship with Him we have to be consciously acting in *faith*.

Where faith is active, the teaching of the Church is experienced as Christ enlightening and guiding: in catechism class, in high-school religious instruction, in sermons and adult education, in papal encyclicals and pastoral letters from the bishops. Where faith is not active, religious instruction may have a positive or a negative effect on us, but it is not an experience of God.

The same is true of the sacraments. Take confession, for example. Some people speak as if for them confession were nothing more than the fact of telling their sins to a man. To reveal themselves in this way may be comforting or frustrating, something they feel a need for or something they dread. But if they experience it as nothing but a human interaction between themselves and a listener whom they enjoy or dislike, then obviously, confession can hardly be for them an experience of God.

Anyone going to confession with an active faith, however, experiences Jesus Christ. There is an encounter. There is a mutual interchange. There is an awareness of personal interaction with Christ. There is a deepening of bond and of relationship. There is the awareness of something lived through together. Friendships are built on moments and memories like these.

Confirmation in believing

This is not just an experience of Christ giving good advice and comfort through the priest. In fact, on many occasions there may be very little of either! It is first of all an experience of one's own belief in Christ; an experience of one's real faith in His incarnational way of dealing with us through the human beings in whom He lives and acts.

In the act of expressing this faith, we are confirmed in our belief. We realize not only that we really do believe, but also that what we believe is real. We experience the truth, the goodness, the "rightness" of our faith when we live it out in action and personal choice.

When faith inspires confession it is an experience of accepting the Church as Christ's real though imperfect Body on earth. It is an experience of believing that Jesus is truly active in His Church, and that He acts on us and for us through His ministers. When we seek reconciliation with Him through His Church, we have the experience of finding Jesus in the sacrament. This is an experience of encounter with Christ; of faith becoming experience.

A disagreeable priest can obscure this experience. A very agreeable priest can obscure it just as much — or even more — by drowning the divine experience in the more immediate consolation of the human.

The experience of God is not essentially an experience of *feeling*, whether good or bad, but an experience of *believing*. In the realization that we believe, we touch on our point of contact with God. When we deal with God in faith we can see, and know, the truth of His action in our lives. This is a different experience than that of receiving merely human comfort from an understanding listener, although the one can work within the other. Both personally and pastorally, the greatest emphasis within the sacramental encounter should be placed on that which fosters living, conscious and active faith.

Celebrating Eucharist with faith

The peak of all sacramental expression is the celebration of the Eucharist. One parish survey revealed, however, that the majority of the congregation did not even come near to finding their greatest experience of closeness to God during Mass. What does this tell us about our liturgy and about ourselves?

Liturgy takes more than tasteful expression and well-planned ceremony. Liturgy is an expression of faith. Where the ceremonies do not mediate the living, conscious faith of the congregation, liturgy will be deadening — and all the more deadening, perhaps, the more exuberant it is.

How many of us listen to the Scripture readings at Mass with a conscious, active faith; that is, believing all the while, as Vatican II teaches, that at that moment God himself is speaking to our hearts? (See the *Constitution on Divine Revelation*, paragraph 21.)

How many of us actively offer ourselves to God together with the bread and wine when these are brought up to the altar? The bread and wine are symbols of ourselves: they are brought up to be transformed into the body and blood of Christ as we ourselves were transformed at baptism. But how many of us really pray at that moment in response to the priest, meaning it, "that our sacrifice might be acceptable to God, the Father almighty?"

And when the host and chalice are lifted up at the consecration/elevation, how many of us join ourselves consciously to Christ lifted up on the cross, knowing that we are really present "in Him" to the Father at the moment of His sacrificial offering?

When we approach Communion, do we go with anticipation, knowing that Jesus Christ is giving himself to us for intimate, personal encounter? Do we truly "commune" with Him during the time of His sacramental presence within us?

No interaction with Christ is an experience of relationship unless it is conscious. Our friends are not just people we know; they are people we *know* we know. That is why it is important for us to bring an alert, active faith to all our moments of encounter with Jesus Christ. Sacraments received routinely do have an effect; but they are not an *experience* of relationship with Christ except in the measure that we receive them with a conscious realization of what we are doing.

Finding Christ in others

Community experiences have fanned to life the faith of many Catholics, both young and old. For youths the setting may have been the Search program, or Teens Encounter Christ, or something similar. For adults it may have been the Cursillo, the Charismatic Renewal, Marriage Encounter, or one of the parish renewal programs which involve group sharing and testimony. These community experiences foster the expression of living, personal faith.

Expression is the key. The faith that is allowed to express itself discovers itself — and reveals itself to others. Faith is like a flame: once it breaks out it spreads. It ignites everything around it. Kept smoldering in the heart it might continue to exist indefinitely — on a survival level — but it will not inflame the world. It will not even give light to "those who are in the house" — to one's personal life, family life, intimate circle of friends.

We have the experience of encountering Christ in others when we approach them on the level of faith, deal with them on the level of faith, open ourselves to them on the level of faith.

To do this, however, with any depth and authenticity at all, we must be dealing with Christ himself directly. To recognize Christ in others we must have some familiarity with His face, the tone of His voice, the nature of His preoccupations. To encounter Him in the "breaking of the bread" we need to have walked with Him along the road, letting Him explain the Scriptures to us while our "hearts were burning within us" (see Luke 24:13ff.).

Finding Jesus in our own life

The Jesus whom we meet in others, who responds to us with life-giving power through the sacraments, who teaches with the assurance of authority in the Church (see Matthew 7:29), this same Jesus is dealing constantly with each one of us individually in our hearts. He does this through His *Spirit* poured out within us.

It stands to reason that the gift of the Spirit is not an inert load. Jesus promised that the Spirit within us would be active, and that His activity would be for us an experience of Jesus himself alive and present to us (see John 14:23ff.; 15:26ff.). What attunes us to the Spirit, however, and makes us able to recognize His voice, His movements, His inspirations within us, is familiarity with the human self-expression of Jesus on earth. To know the human words of Jesus, therefore — to be familiar with their tone, their spirit, their content — is to be familiar already with the language the Spirit will speak in our hearts.

The question of friendship with Jesus comes down to a very human one: "How do you interact humanly with Jesus?" What human words do you speak to Him? What human words of His do you take seriously? How much do you think about them? What words of His have you accepted so deeply that you are building your life upon them? How much time do you spend with Him? When and where? In what ways do you treat Him differently than you treat your other friends? In what ways do you treat Him the same?

In what human actions do you express your faith that Jesus is living and acting today in His Body on earth, the Church? That He is teaching? Healing? Sanctifying? When and where does He perform these ministries in His Church?

How much faith do you bring to your encounters with Jesus in the sacraments? In the eucharistic celebration? In other people?

Evangelists frequently ask, "Have you accepted Jesus Christ as your personal Savior?" Might the Catholic question be rather, "Have you accepted Jesus Christ as living and acting and saving you now through your human interaction with Him in His Church?"

If that is the question, how is the answer manifested in your life?

PART TWO

Reconciliation And Spiritual Growth

The call to be a disciple

CHAPTER 3

A Conversion To Growth

Living the Sacrament of Reconciliation every day

The first sacrament we receive — baptism — is an entrance into *relationship with Christ*. This is a relationship of *friendship*.

Jesus is not just an ordinary friend, however. He is a friend who saves. Everything Jesus is and does for us is characterized by this. Baptism, therefore, is essentially an acceptance of Jesus as *Savior*.

If our salvation were something we received in complete passivity, perhaps we could accept Jesus as Savior and leave it at that. But our salvation is not just an act of power on the part of God. It also involves cooperation on our part. It is a process of growing into complete likeness to Christ.

The salvation Jesus came to give is not just forgiveness of sins. It is the fullness of life, both human and divine. "I came that they might have life," Jesus said, "and have it to the full" (see John 10:10).

Life grows to fullness. It doesn't happen all at once. A process is involved. Salvation, therefore, consists in growing into that fullness of life, both human and divine, which is found in Jesus Christ alone. We do this by growing into complete likeness to Him: into total conformation to His mind and heart and will; into complete surrender to His mission, His desires, His initiatives in our life.

To really accept Jesus as Savior, therefore, means we must go one step farther and accept Him as *Teacher*.

Jesus is the Teacher who forms our total being. He is

the "Master of the Way," our guide along the path of life, the one who forms us by word and example into that "new man" St. Paul talks about. This new man is none other than "Christ come to full stature" — that is, Jesus the Head together with us, the members of His Body, who enjoy the fullness of life "in Him" (see Ephesians 4:13; 5:24).

To accept Jesus as Teacher of Life, then, means to commit ourselves to *discipleship*. The sacrament which brings discipleship into our daily lives is *Reconciliation*.

A sacrament of movement

The Sacrament of Reconciliation is an abiding sign in the Church which calls us to convert more deeply to Jesus every day. We don't actually receive the Sacrament of Reconciliation every day, but we should make *use* of it every day by growing daily in the conversion of mind and heart and will to which it calls us. How can we do this?

The first thing we must do is use confession effectively. Confession used only for forgiveness is a conversion *from*. Confession used as a guide and incentive to spiritual growth is a conversion *to* a more insightful, radical, authentic following of Jesus Christ; that is, to discipleship. If we really believe in Jesus as "Master of the Way" and Teacher, not just of "religion," but of life, then we believe that He can teach us, better than anyone else, how to find what we are really looking for in every area and activity of our lives. "Religion" suggests to us one limited area of life. If Jesus is just a Teacher of "religion," we don't think of Him as having anything positive to teach us about how to enjoy ourselves on a date, be truly successful (as whole human beings) in our business life, make our family lives happy and life-giving for everyone in the home, and bring about peace and justice through politics.

If Jesus is just a Teacher of "religion" for us, we look to Him for rules, for doctrine, for observances, for things connected with "church." If Jesus is the Teacher of Life for us, we look to Him for light and guidance in everything we do.

The Sacrament of Reconciliation is a help to do this.

Confession: an evolution from return to concern

In the earliest days of the Church, Reconciliation was a public re-integration into the Christian community of someone who had left the community of believers by denying the Faith. A person, for example, who publicly denied Christ under torture in time of persecution, could hardly expect to just walk back into the circle of believers after the police released him and take part in the worship service as if nothing had happened. There would have been a credibility gap.

In order to be accepted again as a sincere, authentic believer, the one who had apostatized had to admit that his denial of Christ was wrong; that it was a sin, a moment of weakness, something he regretted.

Through his *confession* of sin his *profession* of faith could be believed. Then the bishop — who alone was empowered to speak for the whole community — would receive him back into the community of the believers. This was absolution.

What absolution expressed and accomplished was a visible reconciliation with the Church, the community of believers on earth. But since the Church *is* the Body of Christ, the true reality of Jesus living and speaking on earth today, reconciliation with the Church on earth was and is reconciliation with Jesus reigning in heaven. Visible reconciliation with the community through confession and absolution is at the same time invisible reconciliation with the Lord Jesus and with the Father.

In the first days of the Church the Sacrament of Reconciliation was celebrated as an expression of *return*. Later it began to be celebrated also as an expression of *concern*.

As time went on, people began to have some doubts about the reality, the sincerity of their relationship with Christ, not because they had denied the Faith, but because they were doing some things which seemed incompatible with authentic faith and love.

Reflection on the Gospel had begun to sharpen consciences. Things which had always been taken for granted in society now began to look like a denial of Christian ideals — implicitly, therefore, a denial of the Faith. Slavery would be a striking historical example of this; and in our own time segregation.

Already in the earliest times the Church had recognized

murder and adultery as sins which called for public reconciliation with the community. As time went on, individuals began to ask themselves if other things they were doing — things no one knew about, perhaps — were not just as much an implicit denial of the teaching and principles of Jesus. They began to wonder whether they might have actually denied the faith through their manner of living while continuing to profess it through religious observance.

In their concern about the state of their souls, they consulted monks: holy men given to prayer and fasting, whose advice they felt confidence in. The monks in many — perhaps most — cases were not priests. What they did was coach their penitents through a long process of conversion. They helped them seek the causes of their sins: the distorted attitudes, false values, wrong priorities, unconquered appetites or destructive desires which were the roots of their bad behavior. And they prescribed remedies: ways of praying or of doing penance which would attack and heal the evil at its root. When the process seemed reasonably complete and the penitent's "conversion" appeared to be an accomplished fact, the monk and the penitent celebrated together the restoration (or the reformation) of the penitent's relationship with God.

Eventually the Church combined these two ways of dealing with sin: the public, official act of reconciliation with the community, and the private, personal process of conversion and repentance. The bishops empowered the priests in their dioceses to speak officially in their name and to declare publicly reconciled with the community those penitents who came to them in private. They gave the priests the power to grant absolution.

By this act the Church encouraged people to use the Sacrament of Reconciliation privately as a means of *growth*, revealing their whole hearts in confidence to someone who could give them advice and coach them in conversion. At the same time she made the private process a means to public reconciliation and forgiveness. The Sacrament of Reconciliation thus became a sacrament of growth and discipleship.

In our day, unfortunately, the focus on conversion, healing, and coaching to reform has to a large extent been lost. People go to confession just to "receive absolution," understanding this as nothing but an act of forgiveness on God's part — as if the only thing needed were for God to change *His* mind and not be mad at them anymore! The "penance" assigned by the priest is not a real remedy but a token gesture of reparation. People go to confession not to begin a process of deeper conversion, but simply to put an end to their guilt and fears.

We can, however, choose to use confession on a regular basis as an ongoing sacrament of growth. If what we seek in confession is a deeper, clearer understanding of our relationship to Christ, of how faithfully we are living by His word and example in all of our decisions, with the intention of becoming better, then the Sacrament of Reconciliation can be for us a sacrament of continual conversion.

If we use Reconciliation this way, then every time we go to confession we reaffirm our faith in Jesus as *Teacher* and our commitment to learn from Him as *disciples*.

The Gift of Knowledge

The Gift of the Holy Spirit which accompanies the use of this sacrament is *knowledge*.

Knowledge is the gift of "practical know-how" in the spiritual life. By the Gift of Knowledge we see how all the ordinary, human things in our lives contribute to or interfere with our response to God. By knowledge we are enabled in confession to call things by their right names. What we may have seen as "impatience," for example, when we were preparing for confession, might appear to us in the course of our dialogue with the priest to be essentially a lack of trust in God. We were failing to trust, and therefore we were uptight, snappy and impatient with everyone around us. As we recognize what was the matter, we find new clarity, new courage, new hope.

The Gift of Knowledge helps us bring our spiritual experience into focus. By letting us see more clearly how elements in our life-style have been affecting our relationship with God — and our experience of relationship with Him — knowledge helps us to understand what we have been living through.

Perhaps we have felt discouragement because of an inability to overcome impatience. None of our efforts have been successful; none of our prayers have been answered. God seems remote and uncaring — if He exists at all! But in the course of confessing our experience of impatience we realize that our real sin was a lack of trust.

Now we understand why we were unable to change: we were not working on the real sin. We were not even praying for what we really needed! As we see more clearly what has been happening, and how each element in our experience has been affecting our spiritual life, we are strengthened in faith and in hope.

The Fruit of Faith

This example shows us how through Reconciliation and the Gift of Knowledge we grow in *faith-experience*.

This may be a legitimate translation of the "Fruit of the Spirit" named by St. Paul as *"faith"* (Galatians 5:22). As we get more clearly into focus what God has been doing in our lives, and just what the nature of our response to Him has been, it becomes easier for us to believe that God is real, and that something is going on between ourselves and Him. This is a fruit of knowledge and a fruit of the Sacrament of Reconciliation. It encourages us to *fidelity*, which is another translation for this fruit of the Spirit.

What discourages us in the spiritual life and causes us sometimes to call our belief into question is the feeling we have "lost the picture." We aren't sure what God is for us anymore or what we are for Him. It isn't just that nothing seems to be going right in our spiritual lives; it is more that nothing even seems to make sense. If we had a specific problem identified, perhaps we could zero in on it and solve it. But we don't even have enough clarity to know what is wrong. We have just lost the picture.

The Sacrament of Reconciliation is a remedy for this. Through the Gift of Knowledge which operates in the sacrament, we are frequently able to get our relationship with God back into focus again. This is especially true when we make use of this sacrament on a regular basis. Then we live in a more constant enjoyment of the fruit of Faith: our relationship with Christ, His action in our lives, the reality of our response to Him — all these seem almost evident to us. Then faith-experience becomes a characteristic of our lives. This is a fruit of the Spirit.

Liturgy of the Word: a celebration of discipleship

We celebrate our call to discipleship in the *Liturgy of the Word*. This is a communal proclamation of our faith in Jesus as the Teacher of Life.

When the Scripture readings are read at Mass, it reminds all of us that we are called to be "students" — disciples — of the mind and heart of Jesus. We give attention to His teaching, to the message of His life. We read His word.

This reminder encourages us to read and reflect on the Scriptures personally in order to absorb what is there. God's word is too deep, too challenging, too inconceivable in the consolation it offers, for us to absorb it during the three readings at Mass. We need time to reflect on what we read and apply it to our lives. We can do this privately at home, or together with other members of our family, or with friends in a discussion group. But every time we celebrate the Liturgy of the Word at Mass it reminds us that God's word should be the focus of our attention, the guiding light of our every living day. His word is the basic text of our discipleship.

If we believe in Jesus as the "Master of the Way" whose teaching enriches every activity of our lives, then we will want to read and reflect deeply on His words. We will also want to examine and evaluate our response to His words. This we can do in the Sacrament of Reconciliation, using it, not only for forgiveness, but for clarity, light and growth. In this sacrament we will experience the help of the Holy Spirit in the Gift of Knowledge, and in that "Fruit of the Spirit" which is more vivid, conscious *faith*.

To convert *to* this undertaking is a decision to be a *disciple*.

CHAPTER 4

Can I Communicate With Jesus?

*A menu
of prayer*

As we become disciples of Jesus, we enter more deeply into friendship with Him. This is the fruit (better: it is the essence) of spiritual growth.

The difference between friends and non-friends is that friends know each other. Our non-friends may know *about* us. They may know a great deal about us: how we look, where we live, what our skills are, even the record of our achievements and failures. They just don't know *us*.

Non-friends don't know our most personal thoughts and feelings, our deepest fears, our strongest desires, our most motivating hope. Our non-friends, if they have known us or worked with us long enough, might be able to predict what we will do in a given situation. But only our friends can understand how we think and feel. Only our friends can appreciate our interior response. Are we friends or non-friends with Jesus?

As non-friends we can know a lot about Jesus. We can know His history, His doctrine, the rules of His religion, the theology that explains His nature and mission as God-made-man. We can be experts in knowledge *about* Jesus Christ and still not really know Him, still not be His *friends*.

To be friends of Jesus Christ we have to know His heart. This involves communication with Him on a personal, intimate basis.

First level: packaged phrases

Communication between most people begins non-intimately.

Two people work together and gradually become friends. They begin as casual acquaintances, just saying stereotyped things to one another, like "Hi!" "Good to see you," "Take care." As long as we just speak in pat phrases we are hardly communicating with each other — just acknowledging one another's existence. It can be the same with God.

With Jesus we also begin by saying stereotyped phrases, sometimes not paying any more attention to the meaning of the words than we do to the clichés we use with one another. We begin with *memorized prayers*. As little children we learned through these to speak to God, just the way we learned to speak to people. But if we never speak to God *except* in the set words of memorized prayers, our relationship with Him cannot mature.

Second level: facts

More contact — though still impersonal — is established between ourselves and another person when we begin to exchange *facts* and *information*. We talk about sports, the market, things that come up on the job, world news, other people. We joke and gossip.

With Jesus we reach this level of communication when we become interested in the things that interest Him. We find ourselves wanting to learn, to hear more about His life, His Church, the things He taught and did on earth. We just want to know more about Jesus and the people connected with Him. We find Him interesting: how He lived, what He talked about, how other people responded to Him, how they felt about Him, how they showed it, what effect their relationship with Him had on their lives. We find ourselves reading the lives of the saints and books about the spiritual life. We look forward to classes or talks on religion. Jesus becomes a part of our conversation with others.

When we talk to Jesus in prayer we bring Him some facts from our own lives which we want Him to know about: desires we have and want Him to help us with; prayers for others or for ourselves; sins we have committed and ask forgiveness for; thanks for things He does for us that we have begun to notice.

We deal with Him on the level of *facts* which we feel

are of interest to Him as well as to us, matters of mutual concern. Usually at this point we are praying to Him in our own words. We still use memorized prayers (we will do that all our lives, just as we never stop saying "good morning" to people), but we are not confined to these. We have begun to really talk to Jesus.

Third level: ideas

A real breakthrough takes place when we become interested in Christ's *ideas*. At this stage in our growth we usually begin reading the Scriptures, we start to think, to reflect on what Jesus said and did, because we want to know Him. We take His message seriously. We want to know what He came to tell the world, and what He has to say that has meaning for our lives now. At this point we become His *disciples* — students of His mind and heart — and not just interested followers.

The prayer that corresponds to this level of intimacy with Jesus — if it can be called intimacy already — is *meditation*. Meditation in the Christian tradition means using our *minds* to *think* seriously about the events and ideas in the Scriptures, and our *wills* to make *decisions* in response to what we see.

Meditation for Christians is a very human, natural thing. It can be defined very simply as "reflecting on the Scriptures until we come to some decision which affects our life." Anyone can do it. It is simply a matter of taking the thoughts and words of Jesus seriously, the way we would take seriously the ideas of any friend we want to understand and be close to.

Fourth level: feelings

Meditation persevered in naturally turns into another kind of prayer: the focus in our communication which Jesus changes from ideas to *feelings*. We are not speaking here of sentimentality. It is just that we find ourselves in prayer simply resting more and more in a single desire, or in a felt union of attitude with Jesus. We are conscious of feeling the same way He does about something, of seeing it the same way, of being united in desire with Him, and we just stay there. We are moving into *contemplation*. What we are experiencing is called "affective prayer." This is a union of heart with Jesus that develops out of union of mind and will. It develops out of both of these, yet it includes them both.

In any growing friendship, intellectual discussion leads to a union of heart as well as of mind. Friends who have looked at truth together, recognized it as truth, and embraced it consciously with shared appreciation have more appreciation for each other. Each begins to have a "feel" for where the other is "at." They have a sense of harmony with each other, an intuitive understanding of what each other's reaction to different situations will be. The fruit of the time they have spent together is not just that they know more about the topics they have discussed; they also know each other. They have become friends, "one heart and one soul," as the poet put it. Neither is alone anymore in the way he or she used to be; each has a sense of being augmented in life by the other. Life has become "we" instead of just "I."

This stage of communication with Jesus is definitely intimacy, and it is experienced as such. There is a deeper level.

Fifth level: life

Some people become more than friends. They become identified with each other in what they ask from and give to life itself. They become partners in living, bound up with each other in all they live and work for.

Equivalently they give their lives to one another. From the moment this becomes a reality, there is hardly a detail in either one's life which does not concern the other. They are so much a part of each other that there is nothing which either one experiences that is not noticeably affected whenever the other person changes in any way. They have fused their existences together: life could not be the same for either of them if the other died or if the relationship broke off.

Friends who have reached this level of oneness do not just think alike and feel alike. They have chosen, over and above this, to pool their lives: to live and work as one, as complementary parts of one another. They have embraced the same goal, given themselves to the same mission in life, and teamed up with each other in order to accomplish it. Either one without the other would be a life cut in half.

Marriage is the most obvious example of this, and marriage is the image of the union with Jesus Christ to which each one of us is called on earth.

We reach this level of union with Christ when we have so totally embraced His goals as our own, so completely identified our own interests with His, and come to rely on Him so deeply as our friend, that no detail of our life would escape being affected if our relationship with Jesus were to change.

This is the level of relationship St. Paul was talking about when he wrote, "For, to me, 'life' means Christ" (Philippians 1:21). It is total dedication to His Kingdom, to being His body on earth (see Matthew 6:33; Romans 12:1-20).

On this level the other forms of prayer do not cease. We still say the prayers we learned to recite; we still talk to Jesus frequently in our own words; we still read and reflect on the Scriptures; we still spend time just affectively united with Him in mutual appreciation and desire. But there is more.

In a sense, everything in life becomes a prayer. Everything becomes an experience of oneness with Christ because we are united with Him — in desire and in fact — in everything we do. He is with us in everything we are involved in; and whether we act in a way that is pleasing or (at times) displeasing to Him, we never experience doing anything that He is not a part of. We "find God in all things" because we are looking for God in all things. We are looking for indications of His will, for signs of His presence and activity, for ways to please Him, ways to be His instrument in everything we do.

When we are on this level, then in our real intention and desire every choice we make is an embodiment of the constant prayer of Christ's heart: "Father! Hallowed be thy name!" Every choice is a surrender to Christ the Head of the Church; to Christ who is our Head, whose Body we are. Every choice is an act of harmony with the Holy Spirit. And because this really is the dedicated bent of our souls, whenever we act in disharmony with the Father, the Spirit or the Son, we feel it as a contradiction of our being.

Friends communicate. Communication with Jesus, like communication with any friend, develops through different levels. The question that leads to growth is, "What level am I on now?" This is followed by a second question: "What am I doing to grow on this level and so to grow beyond it?"

The goal of Christian life is not to know *about* Jesus but to *know* Him. The Gospel tells us, "Eternal life is this: to know you, the only true God, and Him whom you have sent, Jesus Christ" (see John 17:3).

To commit ourselves to this is discipleship. It begins with communication.

CHAPTER 5

Is My Interaction With Jesus Real?

*Getting down
to earth in prayer*

Real relationship with Jesus Christ is measured by change. Real relationship with anyone is based on *interaction*, and interaction is defined as something that produces change.

If we are disciples of Jesus, then by definition we should be learning from Him. This is how disciples interact with their teacher. But learning is not complete until it is embodied in behavior. The words of Jesus are words of life; the more we assimilate His words, the more our lives should change.

Oil and water don't interact; when they are mixed together, each remains what it was. Salt and water do interact; when they are mixed together, neither remains the same. When we are in contact with Jesus Christ we have to change. If we are not changing, we are not really making contact with Him.

Jesus is more than our Teacher. He is our friend.

Our most significant friends are the ones who have affected our lives the most. If we look back on the decisions which set the present tone of our life-style, we will probably find that most of those decisions were influenced by some kind of interaction with our friends. What, for example — or who — prompted our decision to start smoking (if we do) or not to start? To use bad language or not to use it?

How did we decide to go to the schools we went to? To get into the kind of work we are in? Who introduced us to the spouse we married? How many of our attitudes, values and ways of behaving have changed since we were married? How much did our interaction with each other have to do with that? Is there any significant decision in our lives that we have made without influence from the people we were close to?

How many decisions can we attribute to the influence of Jesus Christ?

Seeing Jesus in action

Our friends influence our decisions because we *interact* with them. Probably we learn more from our friends than from anybody else. Every friendship is a mutual teaching about life.

We ask our friends' opinions: we observe their reactions, are sensitive to their feelings and judgments; we base a lot of our decisions on the way they decide and choose and act.

We frequently think of our friends when we have a decision to make, imagining what their response would be. We remember things they have said, reactions they have shown in the past. We relive the emotional experience of their approval or disapproval. If their advice to us has proven helpful in the past, we are inclined to follow their opinions in the present.

Do we go through the same human process in our relationship with Jesus Christ? Can our relationship with Him as friend and Teacher of Life be humanly real without it?

Many people say, "But I've never seen Jesus' reaction to anything I've done. I'd have to guess at it." Or, "I could ask Him for His opinion, but I wouldn't expect Him to talk back and give it to me." To interact humanly with Jesus seems unreal. That is because we haven't tried it seriously.

The Gospels show us Jesus reacting to a wide variety of human situations — so many that if we read and reflect on the Gospels until we are familiar with them, we will not have much trouble getting some sense of how Jesus would react to the decisions we are faced with every day. We may not be able to say with absolute certainty what He would do, but then we can't always say that about our other friends either. The Gospels reveal as much about Jesus as our daily contact with our friends reveals about them. Anyone who reflects on the Gospels knows this is so.

That is why it is true to say that ordinarily the choice to interact with Jesus begins with a choice to read and reflect on the Gospels.

Jesus' interaction with us

It is not true that we have never seen Jesus' reaction to anything we have done. We may not have seen it with our eyes, but we have felt it most clearly in our hearts. This is a knowledge as sure as any knowledge can be.

Jesus has expressed His feelings to us over and over again. And we have understood. If we have not recognized more often what He was saying to us, it is probably because we didn't bother to pay attention to the feelings and interior reactions of our own souls. Or we didn't know how to interpret them.

The movements of our hearts are able to reveal to us the way Jesus is responding to our behavior — and not only to our behavior, but to our thoughts and decisions, our feelings and moods, our sadness, our joys and our desires. Jesus expresses himself to us more consistently and more clearly than any friend we have, provided we really invite His reaction and really want to perceive it.

No one likes to intrude on the privacy — and even less on the freedom — of a friend who might resent it. For this reason most people, even our closest friends, often send up weather balloons before they react explicitly to something we have decided to do. They first signal with a slight expression of the face, perhaps; one that can be overlooked. Or they offer a noncommittal comment to begin with. They send us a response we do not have to perceive unless we are looking for one. They know that if we are truly interested in their opinion we will understand the offer and follow up on it.

Jesus does the same. His first reaction to anything we do is usually very low key, almost imperceptible. (We are not talking here about obvious choices to do great evil or great good, but about the everyday decisions we make almost without thinking about them. These decisions nevertheless set the tone and direction of our lives). Jesus is not unconcerned about anything we do, but He does not make His reaction known unless we really want to hear it. The key to our growth toward Him is freedom — free response in love. He gives himself to us because He wants to, because He loves us, and this is the only way He wants us to give ourselves back to Him.

41

Getting down to earth

How, in practical terms, can we make our interaction with Jesus Christ something conscious, perceptible and real?

Electricity only flows between two poles; that is why there have to be two wires to make an appliance work. For our relationship with Jesus to be real — for any real action to take place — we need to run two wires.

The first is a positive wire. It is our connection to the source of power and light. We need to be "plugged in" to Jesus, and the best way to do this is through Scripture. We have to let His ideas, His example, His words, His living voice come through to us. That is the positive wire.

We also need a ground wire. Electricity doesn't move except to flow back into the earth. The ideas and words of Jesus don't influence anybody or effect any change in us until they are brought back to ground through application to daily life. When we let the truth and goodness — the light and life and love — that have come into our heads through Scripture flow back to ground level through concrete decisions which affect our daily living, then His power is moving in our lives. Then there is change. And interaction. And real relationship.

Perceiving interaction

To keep this process going, however, we need a way of keeping score.

That might sound strange in a relationship of love. But love feeds on awareness. What keeps us giving gifts is the realization that they are received. If we were not sure they ever arrived, pretty soon we would begin to fear that we were throwing our treasures away.

Suppose that every time we shot at the goal in a basketball game we had to guess at whether we hit or missed. Suppose we weren't allowed to look: how long would we keep playing basketball?

If every time we wrote a letter we had no way of knowing whether or not it had arrived, because we never got an answer, we wouldn't write letters very often.

And if every time we try to make a decision that is pleasing to Jesus Christ we are left wondering whether it actually does please Him or not — or whether He even notices — we just won't try to please Him for very long. We will stop trying to live personally and creatively by the Scriptures, and we will go back to just living by the rules. Then our religion will be nothing more than the passive subjection of not breaking out of bounds, of not rebelling against God's will. It will not be an active, loving, creative and individual response to the person of Jesus Christ. It will not be interaction. It will not be real relationship. It will not be discipleship. It will be static and dead.

To remain in life-giving relationship with Jesus Christ, it isn't enough to interact with Him; we have to *know* we are interacting. In our efforts to respond to His mind and heart, to follow the inspirations of His Spirit, we have to know, to some extent at least, when we hit and when we miss. We have to see enough results to know if there is any current in the wire.

An "awareness exercise"

The best way to do this is to look back daily on our interaction with Jesus. And the key to this review, surprisingly enough, will be our *feelings*.

We could ask (and should, although it will only help us up to a point), "What have I done today in response to His inspirations, His desires? How have I lived by His word?" These are helpful questions, but they only introduce us to the level of our conscious perceptions. What can be recognized with the head has already been partially processed by our brain.

There is another level of perception — the less conscious but more significant awareness of the heart — which cannot be accessed through thought. The heart is entered through the same door through which it expresses itself: through feelings.

To key into our heart reaction to Jesus Christ we have to ask questions about moods and feelings, about affective motions and changes. "Has my experience of this day been happy or sad? Did it start off one way and then change? What caused the change? When did it take place? What happened just before that?"

Some mornings we begin the day feeling at peace with God and the world. By the time we come home from work we are feeling uneasy, restless and disturbed. If we look back on the day we may be able to pinpoint the moment when the uneasiness began: a word that was said to us, an answer we gave, a decision we were faced with, a thought that passed through our head. This is the moment we need to look at in the light of our interaction with Christ.

It is possible that an uneasiness we feel may come from the fact that unconsciously we are going against the direction Jesus wants us to take. An increase of enthusiasm and joy may be the fruit of following an inspiration which we have not yet explicitly recognized or acknowledged as coming from Him.

All feelings are not echoes of God's action on our hearts, of course. If the stock market has crashed, carrying away my whole life's savings, I don't need to go into any spiritual discernment to explain why my day has just gone bad. Likewise, if I have just made a sale that nets me nine thousand dollars in commission, I don't have to interpret my joy as a consolation from God (although I might see the sale as His gift). But even when the source of an emotion is clear, almost any feeling can be a starting point in my effort to clarify communication with God. And when I don't really know what has caused a change of mood, there is even more chance that through looking into my feelings I might discover some discreet whispering of the Spirit in my heart.

Sometimes we need the help of a spiritual director or of some other experienced person to discern what our feelings are telling us about God's action in our lives. But on a day-to-day basis, if we just try to listen to the movements of our hearts and examine them in the light of what we already know of Christ, we will find ourselves growing familiar with His voice.

It is through this kind of reflection, especially when it becomes a regular part of our lives, that we come to know whether the light and power we receive through our meditation on Scripture is getting back to ground level — back to the ground level reality of our concrete, daily decisions. When we see that it is, and that our lives are changing through our response to Jesus Christ, then we know that our relationship with Him is real. Then we know that we are His disciples in deed and truth, and not only in name.

PART THREE

Confirmation And Christian Maturity

The call to be a prophet

CHAPTER 6

A Conversion To Maturity

Living the Sacrament of Confirmation every day

One of the greatest conversions in life is the acceptance of adulthood. Adulthood is a change. It is an experience. And it is too often missed as an explicit moment of acceptance.

The transition from childhood to maturity is a key moment in anyone's existence. In most civilizations this transition is actualized in an *initiation* ceremony. This "rite of passage" celebrates two things: an individual's explicit, free, deliberate *conversion* to the state and responsibilities of adult life; and the community's *acceptance* of the individual as a mature, adult member of the group.

In the spiritual life, as in physical and social life, there is a stage of childhood and a stage of adult response. We celebrate the passage from the one to the other in the Sacrament of Confirmation.

The celebration of this sacrament — if we understand its authentic meaning — is a real act of conversion, both on the part of the individual, and on the part of the faith community to which he belongs. For the individual receiving Confirmation it is an expression of *commitment*. For the community conferring it, it is an act of official *acceptance*. With the reception of this sacrament a person's status in the Church is changed. So is his relationship with Christ.

In the early Church baptism and confirmation were not distinguished. The baptized were all adults, and so they were initiated at baptism directly into adult Christian life. As time went on, however, and infants began to be baptized, the Church realized that an infant can only be initiated into infant Christian living. An infant cannot do anything as an adult, whether on the plane of nature or on the plane of grace. An infant is an infant. A child is a child. When the children became adults, therefore, they needed to be initiated into the ways and responsibilities of mature Christianity. They needed to recognize and accept the change in their relationship to Christ; that they were no longer children in their interaction with Him, but free and cooperating adults. They needed to understand what this involved. And the community needed to accept them as changed — as being children no longer, but adult members of the Church. This is what Confirmation is: the sacrament of initiation into adult Christian living.

Work spells the difference

The difference between a child and an adult is that adults contribute to society, while children only receive.

On the biological level we are mature when we are able to give life. When our bodies have developed enough to reproduce, the transition has been made. Before that, nothing is asked of the body except that it should grow and develop.

On the sociological level we are considered mature when we are accepted as able to *go to work*: to contribute to society, to do our part, to take on the full responsibilities of membership in the group.

Children are not expected to work. The basic duty of children is just to grow: to take in, to absorb, to learn, to make themselves ready for adult life. When a child is pronounced mature it means that he or she is ready to give back to society as well as to receive. Adulthood means the ability to give life, to work, to be productive, to contribute one's share to the development of the world and the good of the human race. In the Church it is the same. Children in the Church are only asked to keep the rules; to obey; to learn; to grow into a mature understanding of the Faith (see Galatians 3:25). Adults, however, are asked to take up and carry on the mission of Jesus, the work of the Church on earth. Adults are asked to bear *witness*.

Words made flesh in action

Witness is the essential work of Christianity. Whatever else we do — whether in family or business life, personal or public activity — we are called to do it as an expression of the continuing presence and action of Jesus Christ on earth. Jesus is risen; we are His Body.

Whatever we do, we are sent to do it as the risen Body of Christ. His life, His love are embodied in us; we are His continuing presence in the world. In us, through us and with us He continues to carry on His work. (See Matthew 9:35 to 10:42; 28:16-20; John, Chapter 17)

There are two things to notice about witness: first, it is primarily a matter of *action*, not of words. Secondly, it must be manifestly *personal* to be effective.

This means that our witness to Jesus is essentially faith *embodied*, hope *embodied*, love *embodied*. We bear witness to Jesus when the words of Jesus take flesh in our actions. Jesus is the Word of God made flesh; the outward manifestation of His presence in us is that we give flesh to His words. (See John 14:8-26)

The definition of a prophet

The sign that our faith, our hope, our love, have become *personal* is that we go beyond the rules.

To bear witness to Jesus as we should, we must do more than keep rules. We show that we have personally embraced the rules, the mind of Christ behind them, the goal that they aim at, when we begin to observe the law of God creatively. In the measure that we do this we live up to our baptismal consecration as *prophets*.

A prophet is one who sees how to apply the word of God to the concrete circumstances of his own time, place and culture. The prophet "gives flesh" to the word by living it out in action. He embodies the Gospel in his life, giving it reality in space and time. And he does this by seeking out new and creative ways to apply Christ's words to the reality of his own time.

The prophet does not just do what he has been taught to do. As a mature and adult Christian he also contributes to the Church's understanding of the Gospel by *making connections* between the words of Jesus and the lived, concrete, down-to-earth reality of modern family and social life, business and politics.

In this way he shows that the Word of God has become a part of his personal reality; that he is personally, freely and deliberately trying to walk by its light, to make decisions according to its direction and spirit; to live out the words of Christ in love.

To take on the work of prophetic witness is to accept Jesus as *Leader* and *Head* of His Body on earth. It is to enter into mature Christian life as a co-worker with Christ and load-bearing member of the Church. This is a significant act of conversion.

The Gift of Fear

The gift of the Holy Spirit which helps us make and persevere in this act of conversion is "Fear of the Lord."

This gift has a misleading name. It does not make us "afraid" of God as we understand this term. The essence of fear is not the emotional state of fright, but simply *perspective*. Fear helps us to appreciate danger, to see in proper perspective anything which threatens our life or well-being.

The recognition of danger is based on a perception of what is for our good. Fear of the Lord, therefore, is called the "beginning of wisdom," or the first awareness we have of how good God is for us.

By the divine Gift of Fear of the Lord we appreciate God for what He is. We recognize that God is All. He is not simply greater than everything else: He is great beyond all values. He is God. He is our survival. All life, all the good we can hope for is found in Him. Apart from Him there is nothing but destruction.

This is appreciation, not terror. And the gift of fear which helps us choose God and avoid sin is also appreciation. It is the gift of evaluating God in terms of our own survival and need. By this gift we realize with absolute clarity how God weighs in the balance of our good. We see that all our good, all our survival, all our fulfillment in life simply depends on union with Him; is identified with Him. And consequently that anything which threatens to separate us from God is the very definition of danger; it is the only absolute menace.

This is Fear of the Lord: the gift of getting survival into perspective.

A truck driver isn't "afraid" of the highway. But he would not drive down the left side of the freeway at night with his lights off just to prove he is not chicken! Any driver knows that to go against traffic is destruction. In the same way, by the gift of fear we are not "afraid" of God, but we would not dream of acting contrary to His will. God is traffic you just don't go against!

Fear of the Lord is the gift of the mature. In little children it might take the form of fright, but then the gift of fear cannot be what it should be. In little children fear is more emotional than rational; but the Gift of Fear of the Lord is not an emotion. It can be its authentic self only in those who are mature.

Children aren't always able to see things in perspective rationally; it often takes fright, fear of punishment, to get them to do what is for their good. "Ships and children are steered from behind." But adults act out of a perception of what is helpful or harmful to them. The emotion of fright does not normally enter into it. The same is true of Fear of the Lord: in mature Christians it is a divine "survival instinct"; but it is not emotional fear.

When Fear of the Lord reaches maturity, its effect is not just to strengthen us in the negative obedience of "keeping in bounds." It also impels us to the positive obedience of whole-hearted *dedication*. The positive effect of Fear of the Lord is to move us to surrender our whole selves to God in reverent obedience and service. Jesus is God: all our good is found in surrender and service to Him. And this is what Confirmation commits us to: the adult service of God.

The Fruit of the Spirit: peace and self-control

The Fruit of the Spirit which follows upon Fear of the Lord is the double fruits of *Peace* and *Self-control*.

Peace has been defined by St. Augustine as "the tranquility of order." Fear of the Lord, by helping us surrender to God as God, puts order into our lives and therefore peace.

The fruit of self-control (or in some translations, "chastity") is a particular consequence of Fear of the Lord, because the Gift of Fear strengthens us to resist the allurement of pleasures and other apparent goods when these go contrary to God's will. (The Gift of Fortitude helps us to take on what is difficult; the Gift of Fear helps us to resist what is attractive.) This is an obvious aid to self-control.

But self-control is also a logical consequence of Confirmation in another way: Confirmation is the sacrament which dedicates us to the *mission* of Jesus. People who have personally embraced a goal find it meaningful — even easy — to take the means which lead to the goal. This is not true of those who are just doing what they are told because they have been told to do it. That is why children have to be constantly reminded and pressured into doing things (like brushing their teeth or going to school): they have not yet personally understood or adopted the goals to which these things lead. When they themselves make the connection, and desire the goal, then they are able to discipline themselves.

Confirmation, by being an act of personal dedication to the service of God, makes it easier for us to do those things which that dedication calls for. We see all the acts and obligations of our religion as helps to establish Christ's reign on earth. Having personally embraced the goal, we have a personal enthusiasm for the means. We serve Him now, not as unmotivated children, undedicated and uninvolved, but as friends and partners. This gives us the momentum of heart we need to persevere in discipline and self-control.

The Offertory of the Mass: a Catholic altar call

We celebrate the adult dedication of our lives to Jesus in the *Offertory* of the Mass. The Offertory, or *Presentation of Gifts*, is the first act of the "Liturgy of the Eucharist." It is also the "Catholic altar call."

In some Protestant churches, after the reading of God's Word and the preaching, the people are invited to come up to the altar and dedicate themselves to Jesus Christ. In the Catholic celebration it is presumed that all those present have already done this through the Sacrament of Baptism. That is why, in the early Church, all who were not yet baptized were asked to leave after the homily: the Liturgy of the Eucharist is an expression of self-oblation "in Christ" and with Him. It only makes sense to participate in it if you have been given to Christ and incorporated into His Body through baptism.

Baptism does, in fact, express the total gift of oneself to Jesus Christ: the offering of one's body (and of all that one does in the flesh) as a "living sacrifice" to God (see Romans 12:1-2). We cannot always presume, however, that every baptized Catholic has made a fully conscious, explicit, personal and adult dedication of his whole life and being to Jesus Christ, just because he has been baptized. Even Confirmation often fails to be, psychologically, the act of personal dedication which it expresses and which, in its spiritual reality, it actually is. At the Presentation of Gifts, therefore, each person participating in the eucharistic celebration is called upon to make this act of self-oblation again, and to make it with ever-deeper and more personal intent.

The bread and wine represent each person in the congregation. As they are brought forward and laid upon the altar to be transformed into the Body and Blood of Christ, each person in church silently presents himself in the readiness of his heart to live and act as Christ's Body on earth in obedient surrender and service to Jesus the Head. Each one offers himself to be transformed. Each time we do this it is a deeper acceptance of our baptism, and an explicit recognition of that adult status in the Church to which we were consecrated by Confirmation. If the Introductory Rite of the eucharistic celebration recalls our first exposure to the Good News, and the Liturgy of the Word invites us to study it, the Presentation of Gifts expresses our commitment to be that Good News made flesh and embodied for the world. In the Offertory of the Mass we offer ourselves to bear witness.

A new standard of morality

Confirmation commits us explicitly to a new standard of morality. Once we have accepted adult status in the Church, we should never ask again whether an action is right or wrong. That is a question for those who are only committed to obeying the law. For those who have taken on the work of the Church and the mission of Jesus Christ, the only relevant question is whether or not a particular way of acting bears witness to the Gospel of Jesus Christ. This is the standard Jesus lived by, and it is the only standard of morality which makes sense for those committed to being His Body on earth.

To convert to this; to accept bearing witness as the criterion for every moral choice we make — for every decision about our life and life-style — this is to accept the meaning of Confirmation in our lives.

It is also what it means to be a *prophet*.

CHAPTER 7

Does My Life Bear Witness To Jesus?

Living in the intimacy of the Spirit

Friends reflect each other. Does my life reflect the knowledge, the intimacy that I have with Jesus Christ?

No one has ever been more intimate with the Father than Jesus. And Jesus was able to say to His disciples, "Whoever has seen me has seen the Father" (John 14:9). St. Paul could say in his turn, "Be imitators of me as I am of Christ" (see 1 Corinthians 4:16; 11:1).

Can I say, "Anyone who knows me knows Jesus Christ"?

People could see the Father in Jesus (whether they were concious of it or not) because in Jesus — in His actions, words, expression — the personality of the Father was unveiled. To know Jesus was to know the Father: to know how the Father loves, responds and cares.

In Jesus the inmost thoughts and feelings of the Father were revealed in human form. They were embodied in human words, human actions, human responses. So united was Jesus to the Father that He said once, "I solemnly assure you, the Son cannot do anything by himself — He can only do what He sees the Father doing. For whatever the Father does, the Son does likewise" (John 14:12).

We glorify Christ in our bodies

Friends reflect each other. The mission of Jesus was to be on earth, before the eyes of men, the perfect expression of the Father. This was how He "glorified" the Father: He made visible on earth the Father's goodness and beauty. Our mission and vocation as Christians is to glorify Jesus as He glorified the Father. Jesus sent us to be the continuing, visible expression on earth of His own truth and goodness. He sent His Spirit into our hearts so that we could do this. He made us His Body, His extended presence in every age and place until He comes again. Before His death Jesus begged the Father to glorify Him in us the way Jesus had glorified the Father in himself (see John, chapter 17). And He makes this same prayer today to us who are His friends.

This is the mystery of our identification with Christ in *grace*. The key to this mystery is *incarnation*.

In human expression nothing is manifest until it is made flesh. Love unexpressed is not recognized; nor has it come to its fullness. The same principle applies to the revelation of God: until the mystery of God's truth and beauty and love is visibly expressed in human flesh, God cannot be revealed as He is. And since nothing less than the human can reflect God's personal life, God depends for His manifestation — for His "glory" — on the human visibility of His friends.

The Father was glorified in Jesus. Jesus is glorified in us. This takes place whenever God's truth, beauty and goodness takes flesh in human actions. This is what grace is: the mystery of God and man united and acting together in one shared life.

When we accepted at baptism to "offer our bodies as a living sacrifice to God" (see Romans 12:1-2), what we really accepted was to let the incarnation of Jesus continue in us. We committed ourselves to letting Him live and love and act in our flesh. We pledged our entire life and action to Him, to glorify God in everything we would ever say and do. We promised to be men and women of the Spirit.

The more we live out this consecration, the more we are witnesses to Him. The more we let the Holy Spirit of Jesus inspire our actions, decisions and choices, the more we "glorify God in our bodies" (see 1 Corinthians 6:20).

Witness in action

As witnesses we continue to be disciples, students of the mind and heart of Christ. But now we are students who can give as well as receive. We have advanced enough to have something to say to the world; something we have learned from Jesus; "what we have heard, what we have seen with our eyes, what we have looked upon and touched with our hands" — or with our hearts (see 1 John 1:1). We are learners who are able to speak. We are witnesses.

We have become familiar enough with the words of Jesus to recognize the voice of the Spirit speaking in our hearts. We have become sufficiently surrendered to His word in our personal decisions and actions to be docile to the Spirit when He moves us beyond the familiar to things we do not completely understand.

Witness, however, is borne in deeds more than in words. In the eyes of God, someone has said, our words have only the value of our actions. In the eyes of men — and in our own eyes — this is also true. We don't believe what people say, but what they do. This puts the emphasis on choices — creative choices.

We bear witness through our decisions; not through anything else. To know the words of Jesus, to repeat them to others, or even to proclaim them from the housetops, is not to bear authentic witness. Only those bear witness validly whose *lives* are a witness to Jesus.

Our lives are this when in actual fact — in ways that are concrete, striking and credible — we live by the words of the Gospel and by the voice of His Spirit speaking in our hearts. We bear witness to Jesus when His words take flesh in our actions; when our lives are an embodiment of His word; when all that we say and do is a "manifestation of the Spirit" (see 1 Corinthians 12:7).

That is why action is the only real witness to Jesus.

The manifestation of the Spirit

Actions, however, do not bear witness to the living Jesus unless they are clearly personal choices. The living Jesus is the Jesus who speaks now, who guides and governs in the Church here and now; who communicates with each individual believer; who inspires through His Spirit every single person who is in living relationship with Him.

The proof of Christ's action in individuals is individual action by Christians.

If the witness of Christians were limited to keeping the rules everyone observes; to living out the Gospel in ways accepted by everyone; to conforming to those patterns of behavior established and approved by the Church as a whole, there would be very little witness to the living Christ. There would be no convincing manifestation of the Spirit, or of the presence of the Spirit in the Church.

A group's established way of life bears witness to belief in something taught. It bears witness to the enduring credibility of a doctrine, to the power of an ideal, to the validity of a principle, to the motivating force of an inspiring example lived out in the past by some great leader. The more conservative a group is, the more manifest their loyalty to a founding father or spirit. This can be true even when their conservatism turns into rigidity and betrays the spirit of the founder.

Christianity, however, is not just a movement which keeps alive the ideas of a dead teacher; or which carries out into practice the inspirations of a charismatic leader. Christianity is the living Body of the living Christ. The community of believers, the Church, *is* Jesus living and acting on earth today. The sign and proof that Jesus is alive in the Church is action inspired by the Spirit of Jesus living and acting in His followers.

The name for such action is *prophetic witness*.

Good news in the world

The essence of prophetic witness is that it be a word of God made flesh. Witness is only given through bodily action on earth. Witness is only prophetic when it is an utterance of the Spirit. When God's word spoken in our hearts takes flesh in visible action, then we are living up to our baptismal commitment as *prophets*. A normal characteristic of prophetic witness is that it "breaks" in some way with the established patterns of the community. To conform to what everyone else is doing — even if what they are doing is perfectly good and according to the Gospel — is either weak witness or no witness at all to the presence of the Spirit speaking in an individual's heart. The Spirit reveals himself through the inspired, personal initiatives of individuals — or through some new direction taken by the community as a whole.

58

Prophets bear witness *to* the Church when they live and act in a way which the believing community itself finds new and exciting (and probably, although not necessarily, disturbing).

Prophets bear witness *within* the Church (to the nonbelieving community) when their way of life breaks with the "civil religion"; that is, with that definition or understanding of Christianity which society finds acceptable and has incorporated into the culture.

It can be taken for granted that any principles or practices of Christianity which are acceptable to the non-believing community fall short of Jesus Christ's ideal. They may be good; but they fall short. St. Paul said that the wisdom of Jesus is foolishness to the wise and clever of this world; that is, to the established, respected, business and professional community; to those whose advice people trust; who are considered solid and reliable by the standards of cultured common sense.

Witness to the Good News is always news — and it seldom appears as good to the wise and powerful of this world. That is why the minimum level of witness to Jesus — when it is witness at all — is to live by the rules.

Law observance, moral behavior, is not to be despised. Sometimes it calls for heroic courage. People have died as martyrs (the word means "witnesses") and been canonized as saints simply for refusing to sin. St. Maria Goretti is an example of this: one of the most modern Catholics to be declared a saint (she was killed in 1902), she resisted the sexual advances of a neighborhood boy until he stabbed her to death. Obviously, when we give up our lives (or our money, or our friends — or risk losing anything that is precious to us) out of fidelity to the law of God, this is striking Christian witness. But in daily life most of us do not find it that risky to keep the law of God as it has come to be interpreted and accepted by the culture. The majority of citizens may or may not live by the same standard themselves, but they respect others who are able to do so. When the values identified as "Christian" have come to make sense even to non-believers, then just to live by those values is no longer a striking witness to Jesus Christ. It does not make obvious our friendship with Him, our intimate understanding of His mind and heart, or our surrender to His Spirit.

59

It is when we go beyond what is commonly accepted that we bear witness. The Good News is not news unless it is new — at least to those who are being exposed to it. Witness, then, is borne by those who have personal insights into the Gospel; who live out the teaching of Jesus in new and creative ways; whose lives are a striking witness precisely because they are more than what people have come to expect from Christians. We bear witness when our lives reflect intimacy with Jesus Christ through His Spirit.

The courage of concrete choice

This is why it takes something more than law observance, good moral behavior, for us to bear witness to Jesus. We have to make manifest His living presence in our hearts by new and personal decisions which have no precedent in law. It is when we go beyond the law, applying the spirit of the Gospel to particular, concrete situations in new and courageous ways, that we reveal the action of Jesus in our lives. This is the witness that bears fruit.

Very often the Word of God does not bear fruit in our lives — and consequently is sterile in the world at large — because we do not let it get down to concrete choices. We hear the ideas and the ideals of Jesus preached; we approve of them in our minds; our hearts are even stirred by them. But we just never take the time — or muster the courage, perhaps — to actually embody them in concrete, personal decisions which alter our life-style.

We don't take the responsibility, for example, of deciding how the Gospel calls on us to restructure our family life; to put our social life on another plane; to set some different goals in our business or student life; to call into question our civic or political inertia. We drift with the current of the culture and by that very fact add the weight of our own lives to its power.

Because we do not have the courage to decide for ourselves how to apply the Gospel to life, the Spirit cannot direct us. Like the tiller on a boat, the Spirit is only effective where there is forward motion. It is true that all motion comes from Him; but when we do not have the courage to launch out into the deep we cannot sense His presence or follow His guidance. Then we lose out on the experience of intimacy with Christ.

To reflect Jesus Christ

Friends reflect each other. This is because they know each other. They share one mind, one heart. They are united in their way of looking at things, in their quality of appreciation and their standards of evaluation. And if they are truly friends, this oneness of mind and heart and ideals takes flesh in action. Their lives reveal the common source of their decisions and initiatives in life. They reflect each other.

Our friendship with Jesus Christ can be measured by the degree to which our actions reflect oneness with Him: a real knowledge and understanding of His heart, a real union with Him in heart and mind and soul.

When our intimacy with Jesus Christ takes flesh in our behavior in new and creative ways of living the Gospel, we show forth the presence of the living Christ in us. We bear witness to Him through the manifestation of His Spirit in our lives.

This is the visible appearance of grace upon earth. It is incarnation.

PART FOUR

Matrimony
And Holy Orders:
The Sacraments
Of Community

The call to be a priest

CHAPTER 8

A Conversion To Community

Living the Sacrament of Matrimony every day

Every act of conversion is a dying to self. At the same time, every act of conversion should be an opening to others in love.

Jesus said, "Unless the grain of wheat falls into the earth and dies, it remains just a grain of wheat" (John 12:24). Dying to self is the key to Christian community. And Christian community is the key to what we are. Our fundamental identity as Christians is to be parts in a single whole: grains of wheat made into one bread; living stones built into the temple of God; members of the Body of Christ. An involvement with others in community is the fastest way to die to self.

Dying to self is also a key to what we are. St. Paul cannot speak of our identity as Christians without reference to the fact that we die in Christ and are called to live as people dead to sin and selfishness, but alive to God and others in love (see for example 2 Corinthians, chapter 5; Galatians 2:19-20; 5:24; Philippians 1:21).

Matrimony is a sacrament which summons every Christian to convert to a deep acceptance of community, and to that "dying to self" whose goal is the perfection of love. That is why matrimony is a sacrament which everyone in the Church is called to live, in and outside of marriage.

Matrimony holds up to every Christian an image of the kind of love to which all of us — the married and unmarried alike — are called. This love is a gift of self which consists in a commitment to "be Christ" and to mediate God to others in "enduring love."

A commitment to self-expression

Matrimony is a sacrament which consecrates two people to form a Christian community in the home for the sake of giving Christ's life to one another and to children. By this very fact, the first thing matrimony commits a couple to is the mutual expression of faith, hope and love. This is a key to all Christian community, and to the very nature of Christian love.

The "common unity" of community is built on mutual expression. People cannot grow to union of mind or of faith unless they express the depths of their thoughts, beliefs and faith-experiences to one another.

Spouses cannot become one with each other on the level of their deepest — that is, graced — being without this unity. Parents cannot form a truly Christian community in the home without it — because they cannot communicate to their children any depth of faith, hope or love to which they do not give some personal expression. Nor can parishes be true faith communities except in the measure that there is a communal expression of faith.

"Community" exists only when, and in the measure that, there is a "common unity" that is conscious to all because it is *expressed.* Community is dependent on comunication. Matrimony, then, is built on a willingness to be "naked" — and vulnerable — to another in the expression of one's heart and soul. And so is every Christian community. This means that every marriage and every commitment to Christian community is a commitment to die to self.

All self-revelation is a dying to self. It is exposure to the risk of misunderstanding, mockery and betrayal. It is also a prerequisite to love. Love requires exposure. Perfect love requires total exposure. Those who fear the risk of being naked to another will never experience the fullness of love. Those who accept it, however, will not only experience love themselves; they can be the mediation of God's love to others. This mediation is an essential of Christian love.

A role of mediation

Matrimony is not just a mutual gift of self made by two human beings. In matrimony Jesus Christ is giving himself to each spouse in and through the other. Every gift of the body in sacramental marriage is a gift of the Body of Christ. Every expression of love between Christian spouses is an expression of the love of Jesus Christ. Every self-revelation is a revelation of the life of Christ. This is why matrimony is a sacrament which consecrates two people in a special way to the exercise of their baptismal consecration as *priests*.

An essential function of priesthood is *mediation*. A priest is someone who mediates the truth and life and love of God to others. This does not have to be the "vertical" mediation of standing between God who is "up there" and people who are "down below." It can also be the *horizontal* mediation which takes place every time we let the God who dwells in our hearts by grace express himself to others in and through our human words, gestures or actions.

When we let God express himself through us in this way, our humanity becomes the medium through which God communicates himself to others, just as He did through the humanity of Jesus. This is mediation, and this is priesthood.

Offered in Christ

It is also *victimhood*. It is dying to self. To let God express himself in and through our flesh without any refusal or resistance on our part is to make a total oblation, a "holocaust," of ourselves. This is to accept in the most total way the meaning of our baptism, when we "offered our bodies as a living sacrifice to God" (see Romans 12:1). It is also to join ourselves to Jesus the *Victim* in the total offering of himself which He made on the cross.

The grain of wheat which accepts to die can become the bread of life. This is the meaning of the Gift of Self to others in Christian community.

Celebrated in Eucharist

That is why the *Consecration/Elevation* is the moment of the eucharistic celebration which expresses most closely the true reality of matrimony.

When the Body and Blood of Christ are lifted up in reenactment of the moment when they were "lifted up" on the cross, all of us who are present join ourselves to Christ in the offering He is making of himself to the Father. This offering is made *to* the Father, but it is made *for* all of mankind.

When we, as "priests in the Priest," join ourselves in Christ in this priestly act of offering, we are being offered with Him as "victims in the Victim." We are saying to the whole world what Jesus said on the cross and what married couples say so explicitly and so dramatically to one another every time they have intercourse: "This is my body, which is given up for you."

An expression of the whole Church

Thus matrimony is not a sacrament which just benefits those who receive it. Matrimony is a reality held up to the whole Church as an image of what Christian love — all Christian love — must tend to be: the total offering of oneself "in Christ" for the life of the world. This love is not only a commitment to community and to the expression (and mediation) of grace to others. It is also, in a very special way — in its deepest essence, in fact — a commitment to *family love.*

Family love is the closest expression on earth of the love which God has shown for us. God has told us that He loves us as our "Father." He loves with the tenderness of a mother:

Can a mother forget her infant,
be without tenderness for the child of her womb?
Even should she forget,
I will never forget you.

(Isaiah 49:15)

Matrimony is the image of Christ's love for His Church (see Ephesians 5:32). Jesus calls us to love and provide for one another as "brothers and sisters" (see James 2:15).

It was only through matrimony — through the family life which has its source in this sacrament, and which we have all seen or experienced — that we first came into contact with the love of husband and wife, of parents and children, of brothers and sisters. It is only through our experience of matrimony, therefore, and of the family life that is dependent on matrimony, that we are able to understand the kind of love which God calls on us to accept and to give to one another and to Him.

Family love is *committed* love. It is *unconditional.*

68

Family members love each other because they are family — not because they have first looked each other over and found one another attractive or pleasant to live with.

No one has to *earn* love in a family; it is given as a free gift. Family members will stand by one another regardless; they will be concerned about one another and give their help to any member in need — just because he is family. This is the kind of love God has shown to us. It is the kind of love He calls on us to give to one another. "Love one another," He says, "as I have loved you" (see John 15:12).

Every Christian finds in family love, therefore — that is, in the love which first comes into existence and is sustained by matrimony — his first experience and enduring model of Christian love. This makes matrimony a sacrament which holds up before our eyes the love every one of us, whether married or not, is called upon to live every day. That makes matrimony a sacrament which speaks constantly to every member of the Church.

The Gift of Piety

It is of the essence of Christianity to love God as our Father and all the redeemed Body of Christ as our brothers and sisters. We are all family. For this reason the Gift of the Holy Spirit which is most appropriate to matrimony is *Piety*.

"Piety" doesn't mean at all what the word suggests to us. The Gift of Piety has nothing to do with sentimental devotion, clasped hands or downcast eyes. It is a gift of loyalty and love.

Piĕtās was the foundational virtue and strength of ancient Rome. It was — and is — essentially the virtue of family loyalty: devotion to one's parents, one's tribe, and to one's tribal gods. As a virtue, piety is the primary "mortar" which holds together all human society.

The divine Gift of Piety is a help from the Holy Spirit to love one's family as sharer in the life and piety of God. This is a piety which embraces the whole world.

For Christians, family love has been extended to embrace the whole human race (see Matthew 6:43-48; 3 John 1:5; Philemon 1:16). We are all brothers and sisters in Christ, children of one Father as "sons in the Son." The Gift of Piety, therefore, enables us to love every man and woman as brother and sister, father and mother in the mystical reality of our common oneness in Christ (see Matthew 15:20; 1 John, chapter 3; 1 Timothy 5:1-2).

This is the Gift of the Holy Spirit which enables us all — married and unmarried alike — to live constantly in the spirit and grace of matrimony.

The Fruits of the Spirit: kindness and patience

The "Fruit of the Spirit" appropriate to matrimony and to the Gift of Piety is the twofold fruit of *kindness* and *patient endurance* (see Galatians 5:22-23).

Nowhere do we find more kindness given to us and more patient endurance extended to our faults than in the home. This may not seem at first glance to be true. The members of our family may yell at us more than anyone else does. We may not find in the home the same considerate, visible courtesy we expect in more formal settings or receive sometimes from total strangers.

But when we go beneath the surface veneer of verbal expression and get down to the bedrock of relationship, it is our families we count on. When we have real needs, our family will take care of us. This is the "kindness" that is real. Home has been defined as "that place, where, when you go there, they have to let you in." This is "patient endurance" without conditions.

At the same time, the Fruits of Kindness and of Patient Endurance ought to manifest themselves in ordinary words as well as in extraordinary deeds! A home filled with the Gift of Piety, where the Sacrament of Matrimony is lived as it should be (by parents and children alike), will be characterized even in external tone and atmosphere by a spirit of loving kindness and patient endurance of one another's weaknesses, woundedness and faults. And this will be a day-to-day experience. Where love is, patience and kindness are gentle. There is thoughtfulness and consideration. There is peace.

The lifegiving power of affirmation

One of the ways in which kindness and patient endurance manifest themselves most redemptively — most productively;

giving confidence, healing and life — is in a spirit of *affirmation*.

It is possible for families to fall — almost unconsciously — into a communal habit of putting one another down. Parents can be constantly nagging their children. Brothers and sisters can be everlastingly at odds with each other: carping, arguing, making negative remarks.

It is true that all of this is very superficial. The parents who nag are expressing — in a counterproductive way, it is true — their deep love and concern for their children. Brothers and sisters who continually pick at each other are nevertheless working from a basis of deep, committed love. Their bond with each other, for example, is stronger than any attachment (no matter how much more emotionally exciting) which they might have with the friends they date or run around with. Brothers and sisters take their commitment to one another for granted. That may be why they express it so little!

Mutual, negative picking can easily come to characterize the atmosphere of the home. It is equally possible, however, to change this atmosphere into one of constant, mutual affirmation. In this the parents must take the lead. Parents who work at it can acquire the habit of noticing and mentioning — constantly — the good things they love in one another and in their children. They can make it their constant joy to "build each other up in love" (see Ephesians 4:16).

In consistent, mutual affirmation among family members, the fruits of kindness and patient endurance flourish and grow. This deliberate, affirming love need not be confined to the home; it can characterize our dealings with every person we know. Then we are living out the Sacrament of Matrimony every day.

A school of "enduring love"

Marriage is a school of love. The goal of every Christian marriage, as of every Christian way of life, according to Vatican II, is "the perfection of charity." This charity is a sharing in the infinite love of God. God described the nature of His love for us, however, in terms of kindness and endurance.

When Moses asked God to prove that He had accepted Moses as His "intimate friend" — to prove it by showing

Moses His "glory," by revealing His inmost self to him — God responded by displaying himself as the God of "kindness and fidelity" (see Exodus 34:5-6).

"Kindness" and "fidelity" (sometimes translated as "grace" and "truth") are from the Hebrew words *hesed* and *emet*. They reappear again and again throughout the Old Testament as a theme song of the divine attitude toward us and of God's own personal nature. They were taken up again by John in the beginning of his Gospel and translated as "enduring love" (John 1:14, 17). What John said was that through Moses God gave His People the Law; but in Jesus Christ He came himself to dwell with us as "enduring love."

The home, then, which is characterized by "enduring love" — and by those Fruits of the Spirit which we call kindness and patient endurance — is a home which reflects the love that is characteristic of God himself. It radiates the life-giving love and presence of Jesus Christ. A family which holds up before its members this ideal — and which lives it out enough to make its beauty visible and its goodness inspiring — such a family is a "school of enduring love;" that is, a school for becoming like God. This is what every Christian community is meant to be.

Our baptismal consecration as priests

In a truly Christian family *priesthood* is constantly being exercised — in each one's constant, loving offering of himself for the life of all. This manifestation and exercise of priesthood is not limited, however, to those who actually are married or live in family. It is the call and the commission of every baptized member of the Body of Christ. In baptism each one of us was consecrated, anointed and sent to be "prophet, priest and king."

Christian love is the total offering of ourselves for the sake of mediating to one another the life of God. We do this by letting the divine life and love which is in our hearts by grace *express itself* in all we do and say. Whenever we do this, we are accepting the place of *community* in our lives; we are accepting *priesthood*; and we are *mediating* God to the world.

To convert to being for others this constant expression and mediation of grace is to live daily in the spirit of the Sacrament of Matrimony. This is a radical act of conversion, and one held out to us all.

It is a conversion to living out our baptismal consecration to be *priests*.

CHAPTER 9

A Conversion To Being Christ

*Living the Sacrament
of Holy Orders every day*

The Gospel is a call to convert to a higher level of life: the level of God himself. This level is not something granted to or achievable by individuals as such. It is a level of life given to a community on earth, and individuals can only attain to it by incorporation into the community. This requires some explaining.

The fact is that no human being can be God — or act on God's level in any way. To know as God knows or love as God loves is simply impossible to any creature. God himself could not give any creature the power to do this. Unless that creature were God himself.

This is what *Jesus* is: a created human nature assumed by the divine person of God the Son. Jesus is God. For that reason He lives and acts on the level of God. Jesus is also human. For that reason, what He does as God is also the act of a human being. But only Jesus is both God and man. He is the "only begotten" Son of God. Jesus alone on earth can know as God knows or love as God loves. He said this quite clearly: "No one knows the Father but the Son. . ." (see Matthew 11:27). Then He added: ". . . and anyone to whom the Son wishes to reveal Him!"

It sounds like a contradiction in terms: Only God can know God. God cannot give any creature the power to know Him as He is. But Jesus says He can reveal the Father to us so that we can know the Father as Jesus himself does. How can He do this?

He does it by joining us to himself. We can know the Father as "sons in the Son." We can know God by being incorporated into Christ as members of His Body, and sharing in Jesus' own act of knowing the Father. Only "in Christ" can we live on the level of God, act on the level of God, or experience anything on the level of God.

Divine life belongs to Jesus Christ alone, and we participate in it only by incorporation into Christ. This is why we said that life on the level of God cannot be granted to individuals as such. It cannot be any individual's possession. It is the life proper to Jesus alone. We can only have it by sharing in His life.

And we do this as members of His Body — that is, as co-sharers along with a lot of other people. The gift of divine life is given to Jesus Christ, Head and members. It is the life of a Body, of many members who are one Body, the lives of many made one.

It is important to notice that when we say "the lives of many made one," we do not mean that God gives His divine life to this individual, then to that one, then to another, and all of these then form some kind of federation or community called a "church." This would be a fellowship of saved individuals. It would not be the Body of Christ. And it would be a contradiction in terms. We have already seen that the life of God cannot be given to any individual as such. Divine life on earth is the life of Jesus Christ. It can only be given "in Him" to those who are incorporated into Him, into the community which is His Body.

In other words, divine life is given on earth to the *community* of the Church, and we share in divine life through incorporation into the Church.

An unavoidable digression

At this point most people get distracted by a problem which should not exist. We live in an abnormal situation. The Church, which is meant to be one visible, organized community of believers, is divided into many communities who disagree on what they believe. And some people do not belong to any church — or at least not to any Christian community.

This is not the place to go into the question of who is and

who is not saved, and under what conditions. For our purposes it is enough to say two things:

First, non-Catholics can be saved. This includes "anonymous Christians" who do not explicitly or consciously believe in Jesus Christ at all. They are saved by a real, if unrecognized, belief in Jesus Christ, and by a real, if invisible, incorporation into the Church, which is the Body of Christ. There are many ways and many degrees of sharing in the life of Christ's Body on earth. We need not go into this further. (Those who are interested will find a good, if brief, explanation in my book *Saving Presence*, chapters 3 and 11). (Dimension Books, His Way, Inc., Memphis, Tenn.)

Secondly, if we want to avoid total confusion, it is best to base our explanation of the Church, the sacraments, and the life of grace on what should be the *normal* situation. If we start with what is normal, with the Church as God intended it to be, and come to some understanding of things, then we can take up the problems and perhaps explain how things work in the actual, abnormal situation of a divided Christendom.

It should be obvious, then, that the only way we can share in the divine life of God is through incorporation into the life of the community of believers on earth, which is the Church. The reason is simple: the Church is Christ. By "the life of the Church" we mean the life of the Body of Christ, Head and members. The only divine life that exists on earth is the life of Jesus Christ, the God-man. We share in His life by becoming members of His Body. His Body is the Church.

Divine life, then, is not something given to individuals as such, but directly to the Body of Christ, and "in Christ" to all who are incorporated into that Body. "In Christ" and only in Him we live and act on the level of God.

Holy Orders: a sign of what we are

The Sacrament of Holy Orders is a sign in the Church proclaiming what we are. The presence of this sacrament in the Church calls all the baptized — clergy and laity like — to live on the level of God. Holy Orders are received as a sacrament only by deacons and priests. The reality expressed in this sacrament, however, is something which speaks to lay Christians directly about the mystery of their own lives.

77

The greatest mystery of Christian existence is that we are not called to be just "followers" of Jesus — followers of His doctrine, of His example, of His laws — but to *be* Christ. The mystery of our being in grace is that we are called to share in Christ's own life and to let Him share in ours: to be His real living Body on earth.

This is the mystery of the Christian community; it is the mystery of every individual incorporated into that community. It is a mystery to convert to. This is a difficult truth to accept, precisely because it is such a mystery.

Aside from the fact that we experience ourselves as being much too human to be divine (how did Jesus himself cope with this?), our mediocrity and our sinfulness make it almost impossible for us to see ourselves as actually being Christ. Being "like" Him to some extent, perhaps; but actually *being* Christ: this is a hard saying to get down! That is where the presence of Holy Orders in the Church is a help.

The actions most proper to a priest are actions which make no sense at all unless Jesus himself is the one who is speaking and acting. If Jesus is not acting in the priest as in His own Body, everything most typical of the priest becomes absurd.

No human being, for example, can forgive sins. If a priest, therefore, says, "I absolve you from all of your sins," then either Jesus Christ is the one who is speaking, or the statement just doesn't make sense. The priest doesn't say, "I forgive you on my part and pray that God does the same." Nor does he say, "After listening to your repentance I am convinced that God forgives you; I reassure you and rejoice with you."

He says very simply, "I absolve you from your sins." If Jesus is not speaking in the priest at that moment, the whole transaction is a farce.

The same is true for the words of consecration at Mass: "This is My Body; This is My Blood." If Jesus is not the one who is speaking, the words are pure nonsense.

When the priest acts as priest, therefore, he acts visibly as one who is Jesus himself. In the priest Jesus continues to speak, to act and to minister on earth as in His own Body. This is what Catholics believe about priesthood. It keeps us conscious of what we believe about the Church. The presence of Holy Orders in the Church keeps us all conscious that the Church herself is the Body of Christ. The Sacrament of Holy Orders is a visible sign of the mystery of the Church. This, however, is also the mystery of every Christian life.

The priesthood of all the baptized

In the lay Christian this mystery does not appear so visibly and unambiguously as it appears in the ministry of the priest. But it is real.

A Christian mother nursing her baby is, as a matter of fact, the Body of Christ. In her, literally, Jesus is nursing the baby. This is a fact. But it is not a visible fact. One does not *have* to be the Body of Christ to nurse a baby. And so in her action the identification of the mother with Jesus Christ is liable to be overlooked.

One does have to be the Body of Christ, however, to change bread and wine into His Body and Blood, and to forgive sins. When anyone performs these actions, therefore, he is explicitly claiming and proclaiming his identification with Jesus Christ. He is also proclaiming the identification of the Church with Jesus Christ: of the Church and all her members. In the ministry of the priest the identification of all the baptized with Jesus becomes visible and is proclaimed.

This identification belongs to us basically through baptism. All who are baptized into Christ are baptized into everything He is. "In Christ" we become both "sons in the Son," and priests in the Priest.

Catholics believe that Holy Orders make a difference. This sacrament confers powers that are distinct, powers which give to the ordained a ministerial function in the Church which is different from that of the laity. There is a real difference, therefore, between the priesthood of the laity and the priesthood of the clergy.

All priesthood, however, is at its root a sharing in the one, the unique priesthood of Jesus Christ (see Hebrews, chapters 5 to 10). He and He alone is Priest. There are no true priests except for those who are "priests in the Priest," and this priesthood becomes ours by baptism. To be *ordained* a priest by Holy Orders one first has to *be* a priest already by baptism. This means it is true to say that in the Catholic Church the laity and the clergy have more priesthood in common through baptism than the ordained clergy have apart from the laity by Holy Orders.

When a Christian woman nurses her baby, therefore, she is mediating God to her child. The baby is literally imbibing the love of Christ at its mother's breast. This is priesthood. But it is not visible like the priesthood of the ordained.

In the visible priesthood of the ordained clergy, the priesthood of all the baptized is made visible. When the ordained priest acts visibly as Jesus still ministering on earth, he holds up to the laity an image and a reminder of what they themselves are. In every action they perform in grace as members of the Body of Christ, the laity are mediating the presence and action of Jesus to the world.

Every act performed in grace is a priestly act, an act of mediating God to others, because every graced act is an act of Jesus expressing himself in human flesh. It is an act in which Jesus and the person performing it are one. In this act the humanity of the graced person serves as the medium, not only of his own self-expression, but of Christ's own thoughts, responses and love.

One like ourselves

Our sinfulness still makes this hard to believe. Here, too, the presence of the ordained clergy in the Church is a help.

Parents frequently feel that Jesus Christ could not possibly be raising their children in them. "He couldn't be! I'm doing too bad a job!"

How good a job does the priest do? If we believe that Jesus Christ is truly ministering in the priest — and frequently ministering badly! — why can we not believe that Jesus is acting in us, even when our surrender to Him is not perfect?

It seems to be a constant throughout history that God does not just call the holy people to be priests. Priests, by and large, are just as obviously characterized by sinfulness and mediocrity as the laypeople are. This is what makes them a sign.

Any lay Catholic who has difficulty believing that in him the living Jesus still acts redemptively for the world need only look to the nearest priest to be reassured! The layman may have sins; so does the priest. The layman may feel keenly his mediocrity, but there is a good chance he will perceive even more keenly the mediocrity of the priest!

And yet, as long as we believe that in the ordained clergy Jesus Christ continues to be present, to minister and to act, we cannot use our own sinfulness as an excuse to deny the fact that we, too, are His living Body on earth and that He ministers in us. Knowing what we are, we just have to try harder to surrender to Jesus as our Head and to live up to our reality as His visible Body on earth. To accept this is to accept priesthood.

The Gift of Counsel

If Holy Orders proclaims to the whole Church that every baptized Christian is called — and empowered — to act as Jesus Christ on earth, then obviously this sacrament points up our need for the Gift of Counsel. Counsel is the gift of the Holy Spirit which helps us know what to do in order to act as Jesus himself would (and wants to act in us) in complex situations.

Not only the need, but the name itself of this gift has a counterpart in secular life. For ordinary living, most of us have enough knowledge of civil law to function. In complex legal situations, however, we take "counsel" — that is, we hire a lawyer. And "lawyer" is one way to translate the word "Paraclete," which is the Holy Spirit's title on earth. *Counsel*, then, is the gift by which our Paraclete gives us expert advice in particularly difficult situations. That is why the laity have special need of it.

What is more difficult than to decide and to act as Jesus himself in the complex world of business and political life, of family and social interaction? To face decisions where there is no simple black-and-white Christian answer is the layperson's "daily bread." It is possible that the normal layperson who is involved in business dealings, social situations, family problems and political compromises has more need of the Gift of Counsel in a day than a monk in a monastery does in a month.

This need is even more evident if we realize that our goal is not simply to do what is "good" as opposed to evil; or even what is "pleasing" to God as opposed to what is neutral, but to do what is "perfect" (see Romans 12:2). This is the kind of judgment we have to make if we are to act as Jesus himself on earth; that is, if we are to let Him live and act in us as in His own flesh, which is what it means to be a *priest*.

The lay Christian, then, has a need to look constantly at the Sacrament of Holy Orders for what it says to him about his own life, and to draw on the Gift of Counsel, without the promise of which no one would have the courage to even attempt to make decisions which are the decisions of Christ himself.

The Fruit of Gentleness

The "Fruit of the Spirit" which goes with counsel is *gentleness*. Priesthood has no meaning except in the service of others. It is inseparable from Christian community. Gentleness, however, holds community together, while harshness breaks it apart.

To share in the priestly mission of Jesus, we must be "gentle and humble of heart" as He was, not crushing the weak, but encouraging them to life: modeling ourselves on the "merciful and faithful high priest" who knew weakness and pain firsthand, who had the touch that healed (see Matthew 11:29; 12:15-21; Hebrews 2:17; 4:14-16).

Not only individuals, but the Christian community itself must be characterized by gentleness. The presence of the priest should be a reminder of this. The ministry of the priest is peace.

Gentleness is normally one of the signs that a person or community is acting by the inspiration of the Holy Spirit rather than by some human compulsion. There are many good things we can do, good causes we can embrace in righteous anger or natural human zeal. But if we are not acting as moved by the Spirit, this often reveals itself in a "tone" of anger or harshness, in an underlying compulsiveness, a negative or critical spirit, an absence of love, or in a positive inclination to violence which accompanies our initiatives.

In the lay apostolate of transforming the world, gentleness is particularly important.

Surrender, not domination

The laity in the Church are specifically responsible for reforming social structures, for establishing the reign of God over every area and activity of human life. In this delicate and potentially explosive work the bond of unity and love between people must always retain highest priority. The Spirit of unity and love moves people to fulfill the mission of Jesus, which is "to bring all things in the heavens and on earth *into one* under Christ's headship" (see Ephesians 1:10). This is the very opposite of that party or factional spirit which wishes to impose its own will, its own way, upon others. The apostolate of reforming society and transforming social structures is either the work of Jesus himself on earth, Prince of Peace, or it is doomed to divisiveness and failure.

Christians do not try to reform the world as superior human beings imposing their own ideals or values on others — regardless of how good or how true these might be. Christians can only act authentically in grace by acting as obedient instruments of Christ. "Apart from me," Jesus said, "you can do nothing" (John 15:5).

But where obedience is, there is gentleness. Where people are acting in surrender to Jesus Christ, a spirit of domination and compulsion will not characterize their efforts.

Jesus alone is the Savior. He alone is the life-giving vine; we are only the branches through which His action is extended to the world. A Christian does not aim, therefore, at doing independently or even absolutely what is good or right, but only at doing what God moves him to do, and in the measure God moves him to do it. Jesus is the Head. Jesus is in control. To be ultimately effective for good, every member of Christ must act, as Jesus did, in obedience and surrender to the inspirations of the Spirit in his heart (see John 5:19; 8:28). The source of Christian gentleness lies, then, in the fact that the Christian is not doing his own will in a spirit of domination, but God's will in a spirit of love, humility and surrender.

Dying to selfishness and self

To act this way is to die to self. It is to efface oneself, to "lose" oneself in identification with another, with Christ. This is why the meaning of Holy Orders (like matrimony) is most appropriately celebrated in the Consecration/Elevation moment of the Mass.

As Jesus is lifted up on the cross — the defeated, triumphing Lord, the Savior/Victim whose scandalous strategy for overcoming evil was, and still is, simply to "endure evil with love" — we who are "priests in the Priest" are called to unite ourselves with Him as "victims in the Victim." We are called to accept dying in Him in absolute surrender so that He might live and act in us to bring His life and love to the world.

To be the instrument of another is to die to self. To be the instrument of Jesus Christ on earth is to be priest. It is to mediate His saving action to the world.

To give ourselves to this work of transforming society as instruments of Jesus Christ is to convert to living out each day the significance of the Sacrament of Holy Orders in the Church. It is to work to establish the *community* of man under the headship of Jesus Christ. That is what it means to live out in lay life our baptismal consecration as "priests in the Priest," mediators of the life of God to the world.

CHAPTER 10

Am I Able
To Talk About Jesus?

*Sharing His friendship
with others*

A characteristic of friends is that they like to talk about each other.

Am I able to talk about Jesus Christ? With whom? How deeply? When do I do it?

Talking is a form of celebration. To celebrate means "to single out for grateful remembrance." This is what friends do. They single out for grateful remembrance special moments they have had with one another, and they relive them by recounting them to others — especially to mutual friends who are able to appreciate what they are hearing.

What moments have I had with Jesus Christ that I like to relive this way? With whom am I able to share, to celebrate, the experiences I have had with Jesus Christ?

My immediate answer might be, "I wouldn't know what to share. I haven't had any experiences with Jesus Christ."

That isn't very likely. All of us have had experiences of Jesus, whether we have recognized them or not. This is true even if we have not been doing much, from our side, to interact with Him. Jesus is always acting on us. He is always trying to enter into deeper relationship with us. It may be that the only way we will learn to recognize His action in our lives — and the real experiences we are having with Him — is to enter into communication with others who have recognized the action of Christ in their lives and are willing to share their experience with us. This is sometimes called "faith-sharing." It is one way to experience Christian *community*.

The need to share experiences

Friendship grows through awareness. Frequently what it takes to bring our experience of another person into full awareness is the act of sharing our experience with someone else. How often, for example, do we start to appreciate someone more after his death because only then do we begin to reminisce and to contemplate in company with others the experience we have had of him or her? As we look back on the special moments when that life touched ours, "singling them out for grateful remembrance," we come to realize how much he contributed to our existence, how much he really meant to us. This is celebration. It is the sharing of experiences. It leads to awareness.

Our experience of Jesus is subject to the same laws that condition our experience of other people. Often it takes celebration — the sharing of faith-experiences with others — to bring our experience of Christ to full awareness.

From moment to moment in our daily lives we interact with Jesus. But frequently there is something left unfinished in the interaction. We speak to Jesus and never take time to notice whether He is speaking back. We ask Him for a favor, for help, and when we receive it we don't recognize that it came from Him. We are not even conscious that our prayer has been answered. Like the nine out of ten people in the Gospel who were cured, we never even think to acknowledge that gift or to thank Jesus once we have received what we asked for (see Luke 17:17). That keeps the favor from becoming experience.

Jesus is constantly guiding our lives, making things come out right for us again and again, and most of the time we aren't even aware He is acting. We never bother to look for or to give explicit acknowledgement to His presence.

A missionary in Africa was late coming home one evening. When he finally returned after dark, the other missionaries asked him what had happened. "I lost my way in the jungle," he said. "I was scared to death. I just prayed that God would show me the way out."

"And did God answer your prayer?" they asked him.

"No, about that time this native came along and guided me home."

When we talk to other people about God, when we share

our experience of Him with them and they share theirs with us, we begin to see a pattern. We recognize from the experience of others that things we had overlooked in our own lives, things we had taken for granted, were really God's intervention, moments of His personal dealing with us. We realize at the same time that we always knew they were — that we were just not bold enough to say so, even to ourselves.

It is a strange phenomenon, but a fact, that we tend to be afraid to admit how good God is to us until we understand that He is constantly being good to other people in similarly beautiful ways. Once we realize we are not claiming something exceptional (just personal, individual and unique to ourselves!), we feel more free to claim His love and consciously acknowledge His action in our lives.

An aid to discernment

Sharing also sharpens our awareness. Once we have recognized and acknowledged God's dealings with us in the past, we are more alert to notice His dealings with us in the present and the future. Our sharing with others gives us a sense of His way of acting, a perception of His personality. As we listen to other people's experiences, our own experience of God is broadened. We are confirmed in what we thought we knew of Him, clarified in our insights, made more confident in our discernment.

Sometimes our misconceptions are corrected. We realize that we have been working out of a false assumption or failing to see the obvious. The acknowledged mistakes of others alert us to our own — or make it less threatening to admit them.

In any friendship it is helpful to have a go-between. Even the best of friends sometimes fall into misunderstanding, hurt feelings, inability to communicate. These are the times when another friend — one who is close to both parties — becomes invaluable.

In our friendship with Jesus it is the same. We need friends who are friends of His to interpret to us at times the way He is speaking and acting toward us. And we sometimes need friends to point out to us the implications of what we are saying and doing to Him.

That is why people who have experience of Jesus Christ,

and who want to grow in closeness and intimacy with Him, invariably thirst for conversation with others who know Him and love Him. Friends need to talk about each other with other friends who understand.

The sharing that turns us off

This kind of sharing is not to be confused with the compulsive gushing of people who just have to babble about their presumed religious experiences. All of us have been turned off at times by people who speak to anyone they meet as if they knew everything about God and come across to us as knowing nothing. Because we don't want to be identified with such behavior, our tendency in the face of it is to draw back and not say anything at all about Jesus or our experience of Him. Who wants to join his voice to a chorus of idiots?

There is an enormous difference, however, between that compulsive sharing, which is really a way of going on and on to another about oneself, and the authentic expression of faith in which Jesus is speaking *through* someone about *himself*. The difference is easily recognized.

When people are just laying on you their latest trip with Jesus, all you are learning is about them. Mostly what you are conscious of is that they have a problem! But when people are sharing authentic experience of Jesus, you are conscious of making contact with the Lord.

In authentic faith-sharing the speaker becomes transparent. This is a way of dying to oneself: to one's self-enclosedness, one's self-sufficiency, one's system of self-defense. To speak from the heart about God is to be stripped: one's defenses are down, the veils are dropped, and one is vulnerable. In the presence of Jesus "the thoughts of many hearts are laid bare" (see Luke 2:35). In real faith-sharing the vessels are broken open so that light might shine forth for the glory of God (see Judges 7:16-22).

In authentic faith-sharing the self is stripped away and the action of God is revealed. This is at one and the same time to make oneself most invisible and most visible. The focus is on the person of God, but one's own person is naked and exposed.

This is why real faith-sharing is not only supportive and

life-giving; it is also an act of dying to self. When others share their experience of Christ with us, it builds us up and encourages us. When we are called to share our experience of Him with others, we do it sometimes at the price of our lives. From the heart that is opened flow living waters. But in the opening there can be blood.

This is the law of community: those who are willing to die to themselves find their being enhanced and multiplied. Those unwilling to die to themselves remain unfruitful and alone (see John 12:24).

An acceptance of priesthood

Faith-sharing is an experience of *priesthood*. To be priest means to be mediator: someone who acts as an intermediary to bring God to men and men to God. This mediation takes place every time we allow the God who dwells within us by grace to express himself in and through our human natures.

Every person who shares by baptism in Christ's character and mission as Priest shares also in His mission to be Victim. We who are "priests in the Priest" because by baptism we were incorporated into Him and into all He is, are by that same fact consecrated to be "victims in the Victim." The only way we can offer Christ to the Father or to others as "priests in the Priest" is to offer ourselves in Him as "victims in the Victim." We cannot give Jesus to anyone without giving ourselves.

To break open the vessel of our own hearts; to let the "fragrance of the knowledge of God" which is within us spread through all the house — this is to be an "aroma of Christ" in the world (see 2 Corinthians 2:14-16 and Mark 14:3; John 12:3). It is a way of living up to what Jesus expects of His friends: "Whoever acknowledges me before men," He promises, "I will acknowledge him before my Father in heaven" (see Matthew 10:32).

To share with others the light and love of God which are within us is an exercise of priesthood. It is also a sign and a proof of our friendship for Jesus Christ.

PART FIVE

Anointing And Eucharist: The Sacraments Of Enduring Love

The call to be a king

CHAPTER 11

A Conversion To Courage

Living the Sacrament of Anointing every day

The sacraments call us to be what we are. Each one invites us to convert more deeply to the mystery of being Christ; to give ourselves more wholly to the mission of living as His Body on earth. How does the Sacrament of Anointing do this? To what specifically does the "sacrament of the sick" call us to convert? Anointing is a proclamation of Christ's triumph. Anointing is given to strengthen us so that we might meet the challenge of death — or of anything which threatens the fullness of our existence (sickness, for example) — with victorious faith, hope and love. It is the sacrament which applies to us in our moment of need the victory which Jesus won on the cross over sin and death. The faith to which it calls us (and which it helps us to actualize) is faith in Jesus as *Lord*. As such, anointing is the sacrament which is most closely associated with the *apostolate* — especially, perhaps, the apostolate of the laity, which is directly concerned with transforming, healing, and raising up the secular life and activity of this world. ("Secular" means that which belongs to this world. Business and family life, social life and politics are all "secular" activities. According to Vatican II it is the lay or secular Christian's specific mission to reform, renew and redeem the secular life and activity of our world. See "Decree on the Apostolate of the Laity", chapters 1 and 2.)

A sacrament of encouragement

Every Christian apostolate is discouraging, because Jesus

chose to save the world, not with a display of divine power, but by "enduring evil with love." Ever since Calvary, Jesus has been triumphing through defeat and overcoming evil within the very experience of weakness.

We may find it easy — or perhaps we are just accustomed — to believe that Jesus has power over sin (in the abstract) and the devil, because these are invisible realities. But it can be mind-blowing to even dream that Jesus has power to reform the social order: to actually make politics honest, business beneficial, family life holy, and social life wholesome. When we know firsthand the clenched hold of evil on the world, Christianity appears to us like David standing before Goliath. We want to say "It's hopeless!" We are afraid to take on the giant.

The answer to this is the presence of *anointing* in the Church. Just the existence of this sacrament reminds us — proclaims to us — that Jesus has won for us the power to triumph over death itself — and through death over sin, which alone makes death a menace. If death itself cannot defeat us, what can? If death has been turned into victory for us, what can be loss? Anointing, by holding out to us the promise of victory over the greatest threat to our existence in this world, strengthens us to confront with confidence every lesser threat. That is why this sacrament is particularly significant for those in the lay life whose apostolate it is to transform secular society.

The apostolate of the laity

Since it is the defining characteristic of the lay state, according to Vatican II, to be "a life led in the midst of the world and of secular affairs," the laity have as their proper, distinctive mission in the Church the job of renewing society according to the light of the Gospel (see the decrees on *The Church*, chapters 4 and 5; on *The Apostolate of the Laity*, especially chapters 1 and 2; and on *The Church in the Modern World*, chapter 4, paragraph 43).

The task of renewing society necessarily brings one into conflict with the culture, with vested interests and with the power structure of the secular establishment. For this reason, lay spirituality is essentially a spirituality of *risk*. It can even be called a "spirituality of martyrdom" (see my book *His Way,* chapters 10-11, St. Anthony Messenger Press).

The lay Christian expresses and experiences his faith most radically and most unambiguously when, by living the Gospel in the workaday world of family and social life, business and politics, he comes into *conflict* with society and *risks* the loss of those goods in which he has invested his life. Risk, not renunciation, is the "name of the game" for those who, according to Vatican II's definition of lay (secular) Christians, live their lives in the ordinary circumstances of family and social life, business and political involvement.

The very existence of the Sacrament of Anointing in the Church gives encouragement and strength to the laity to accept the risks inherent in their life and apostolate. This sacrament is a constant reminder and pledge of the power of God. It promises victory over death itself and over the worst that evil can do. As such it is a sacrament of particular relevance for Christians engaged in the struggle of living by the Gospel in the midst of a hostile world.

The Gift of Fortitude

The Gift of the Holy Spirit most appropriate to anointing is *Fortitude* — the gift which strengthens us to do difficult things or to endure hardship for the sake of the Gospel. It is God's answer to fear.

Jesus is constantly telling people in the Gospel that they should not fear (see, for example, Matthew 10:28; Mark 5:36; Luke 12:32; John 14:1). He urges them instead to have faith, to have confidence, to trust in the Father and in Him. Once a person has overcome the initial obstacles to accepting the Gospel, the greatest block to further progress is fear: fear of losing income, prestige, security, friends, or just control in general. Fear keeps people from bearing radical witness to Christ, from giving themselves without restrictions to the work of establishing His reign over every area and activity of human life. It keeps us from looking with open minds at the call and implications of the Gospel. Fear inclines us to mediocrity.

The Fruit of Generosity

The Sacrament of Anointing and the Gift of Fortitude help us to overcome fear, to live the teaching of Jesus without paralyzing hesitations and restraints, and to give ourselves without timidity to the work of the Kingdom of God. The "Fruit of the Spirit" which results from this combination is *generosity*. Generosity is the attitude by which one does great things for the Lord. It is the contrary, not of evil, but of mediocrity. The generous Christian is not just good; he is magnanimous. He goes all the way in response to Jesus Christ and to the challenge of the Gospel.

Those friends of Jesus Christ who are generous with Him are not timid, defensive, protective of themselves or of their property, prospects or prestige. Those who are generous undertake great things, accept great risks, give themselves without reserves. This is what is needed for the apostolate, and most particularly in our day for the "apostolate of the laity," which is the work of transforming society.

We have already seen that lay spirituality is a spirituality of risk, even of "martyrdom." When we think of the martyrs, however, we don't just think of people who were faithful in observing the commandments. "Martyr" for us is synonymous with "hero." A martyr is someone who is faithful to the point of heroic sacrifice. When anyone gives himself heroically to the risk and the challenge of embodying Gospel values in secular life, this is a manifestation of that fruit of the Spirit which we call *generosity*.

Our baptismal consecration as "kings"

The Sacrament of Anointing focuses our faith on Jesus as Lord: Jesus can strengthen us to confront death or the threat of death fearlessly because He himself has overcome death and entered into His glory. He reigns in power at the right hand of the Father. Death could not keep its hold on Him. He is Lord of heaven and earth. Life and death are in His hands. He will come again in power to unite in himself all of creation in love and subjection to the Father. He is Lord.

Because anointing directs our attention to Jesus as Lord, it calls us to recognize and embrace our baptismal consecration as "kings," that is, as sharers in His Kingship. In practical terms, this is a consecration which commits us to faithful *stewardship*. When we were baptized "into Christ," we were baptized into His triple character and mission as *Prophet, Priest* and *King.* We became "prophets in the Prophet," "priests in the Priest," and "kings in the King."

There is no special word for one who shares in the prophetic or priestly character of another. But there is a word, and one heavily emphasized in Christian usage, to designate one who shares in another's authority as king. The word is "steward." A "steward" is one who accepts the office and responsibility of acting in the name of his master, employer or king. He is charged with the responsibility of looking out faithfully for His master's interests. What is most required of a steward is *fidelity.*

Before Jesus left this world, He called on His disciples to be faithful stewards of His kingship, charging them to look after His interests as Lord until His return. To be a faithful steward of Jesus the Lord, therefore, means to engage perseveringly in the work of establishing the Kingdom of God on earth until Jesus comes again in glory. This is how we live up to our baptismal consecration as *kings.*

This is what the *apostolate* is all about. The Sacrament of Anointing encourages us to engage in it without fear. The Gift of Fortitude strengthens us to confront its dangers and difficulties. Together they lead to the fruit of *generosity* in the service of Jesus the Lord.

Communion Service: celebration of stewardship

Stewardship, like anointing, has an "eschatological" character; that is, it looks forward to the last things, to the end of the world, to Jesus' return in glory, to the final judgment and the eternal reward which is promised to those who are faithful.

For this reason, the portion of the eucharistic celebration which best corresponds to the Sacrament of Anointing — the part of the Mass which focuses on and strengthens us for the faithful, fearless stewardship to which anointing summons us — is the *Communion Service.* This extends from the Lord's Prayer to the final blessing and dismissal.

From the "Our Father" on, the focus of the eucharistic celebration is eschatological. The "Our Father" itself is an eschatological prayer (see Father Ray Brown, *New Testament Essays* [Doubleday]). It is a prayer for the coming of the

Kingdom and of all that the Kingdom entails. The Our Father is followed by a reminder that we should be *waiting* "in joyful hope for the coming of our Savior, Jesus Christ." Right after this we offer each other the Sign of Peace as a preview of the peace and unity of His Kingdom. Then we receive Communion.

Even when we are in perfect health, we always receive Communion as "viaticum;" that is, as the "waybread" which gives us strength for our journey. Communion is the assurance that Jesus is with us now and will be with us to — and through — the end. Communion is God's answer to discouragement. It is a celebration of Christ's victory and resurrection; of His return to earth and His abiding presence among us. It is assurance that He who left us in apparent defeat, and who has left us perhaps feeling helpless and alone, is in fact still with us, guiding and strengthening us along the way. Whenever we feel that we are in a "deserted place" and that "night is coming on," we can find Him in the "breaking of the bread" (see Luke 24:13-35; Matthew 14:13-21; 15:32-38).

A summary:

During the *Introductory Rite* of the Mass we celebrated Jesus as *Savior* — as the one who brings us into life-giving relationship with God. Then, during the *Liturgy of the Word*, we reminded ourselves that He is our *Teacher*, and that we grow to the fullness of life by reflecting on His word as His disciples.

At the *Presentation of Gifts* we offered ourselves with the bread and wine to be transformed. We dedicated ourselves to doing the work of Christ our *Leader* and *Head* as members of His Body on earth. We acknowledged the fact of His ongoing mission in the world and accepted our call, as adult members of the Church, to take an active part in it. We dedicated ourselves to embodying His word and His life in prophetic witness.

At the *Consecration/Elevation* we accepted in faith to "die" in and with Jesus the *Victim*. As His Body and Blood were lifted up, we joined ourselves to Him on the cross for the sake of union with God and with others. We accepted the dimension of community in our lives, our solidarity with others in the sin and salvation of the human race, and our consecration as "priests in the Priest" to mediate the life of God to the world. Now, during the *Communion Service*, we focus on Jesus as *Lord*. We celebrate the Resurrection, which was Jesus' victory and ours. We accept the mystery — and the consequences — of being His risen Body on earth. We encourage ourselves to persevere in faithful stewardship in the work of carrying out His mission, and we look forward to the reward of sharing in His glory as we prepare to go out and confront the challenges of transforming the world. To do this — to deliberately convert to absolute confidence in Christ's final victory, and to show this confidence by carrying the Gospel into every area and activity of human life with courage and generosity — this is what it means to live out the Sacrament of Anointing every day.

It is for this that we are baptized into sharing in the Kingship of Jesus Christ.

CHAPTER 12

A Conversion To Love

Living the Sacrament of Eucharist every day

In Christian tradition the Eucharist is known as "the sacrament of love." It calls us, quite simply, to convert to loving the Lord our God with our whole heart, our whole soul, and our whole mind. This title is as theological as it is devotional; that is, it expresses not just the affection we have for the Eucharist, but the truth we understand about this sacrament.

Love is a gift of self. St. Ignatious of Loyola teaches that love consists in a mutual sharing of what one has or is. In the Eucharist — that is, in the moment of *Communion*, which is what we will be talking about here — what is being expressed and what is happening is just mutual gift. That is why we call it "Communion." It simply invites us to love. In all the other sacraments, Jesus comes to us to do some particular thing:

- In *Baptism* He comes to save us, to incorporate us into His own life-giving death and resurrection, into His Body.
- In *Reconciliation* He comes to forgive and heal us, to help us grow.
- In *Confirmation* He comes to bring us to Christian maturity, to empower us and to send us on His own mission.
- In *Matrimony* and in *Holy Orders* He comes to consecrate us to form the two communities whch are necessary for Christian life to grow to its fullness: the community of the family and the community of the worshiping Church.
- In *Anointing* He comes to assure us of final victory over sin and death, and to bring our response of faith, hope and love to completeness.

But in Communion He just comes to give us himself.

It is true that in this giving of himself Jesus "does" many things for us. In Communion we receive healing, strengthening, and frequently many communications of light and of love. Jesus does not come to us to remain silent and inert. Communion is a very active moment.

Nevertheless, the central expression and reality of Communion is just what the word expresses: communion. It is a time of deep union with the Lord, a time for the communication of all He is to us and of all we are to Him. That is why we call it the "sacrament of love."

Can we accept the value of just loving God? What practical value is there in receiving Communion — just as an experience of love?

The questions may seem ridiculous. Love, we may answer, is an end in itself, not a means. This is true, of course, but the fact remains that the *experience* of love is something of practical value — and precisely for fostering love itself. Married couples know this through the experience they have of sexual gift to one another. Communion is a strengthening of love.

The Gift of Wisdom

We see this more clearly when we look at the Gift of the Holy Spirit which is most appropriately associated with Eucharist. This is the Gift of *Wisdom*.

The Gift of Wisdom is essentially the gift of *appreciating* God and the things of God. The Latin word for wisdom is *sapientia*, which comes from the word for "savor" or "taste." By the Gift of Wisdom we acquire a "taste" for God and for spiritual things.

There are four Gifts of the Holy Spirit which sound like synonyms of one another. They are *wisdom, understanding, knowledge* and *counsel*. It might put wisdom into a clearer light if we show how each gift differs from the others.

In a nutshell, understanding and wisdom help our speculative intellects (by which we have "theoretical" knowledge, or know things just for the sake of knowing them). Understanding helps us to see truth; wisdom to appreciate what we see and to make judgments about it.

Counsel and knowledge help our practical intellects (by which we have practical "know-how," or know things for the sake of doing something). Counsel helps us to see what we need to see in order to decide how to act; knowledge helps us to evaluate and judge what we see in order to make good practical decisions.

Understanding and counsel: gifts by which we see

Understanding gives us insight into the meaning and credibility of revealed truths. By understanding we find it easier to see that a teaching of Jesus is true, and what meaning, significance or message it contains for our lives. Understanding is the gift we associate with the "sacrament of faith" or "enlightenment," which is the Sacrament of Baptism.

Counsel helps our practical intellect see clearly those things which relate to making choices in complex situations. By counsel we see what options are open to us, what principles we should respect, what factors we should take into consideration when making a concrete choice. By counsel we are able to bring together and relate all the various factors of a complicated situation in order to decide what is the more Christian thing to do under the actual set of circumstances. Counsel is a gift lay Christians have special need of as they attempt to live out the meaning of *Holy Orders* — the sacrament which summons us all to be and to act as Jesus himself in our own time and space.

Wisdom and knowledge: gifts by which we judge

Knowledge is the gift of day-to-day, practical "know-how" in the spiritual life. It helps our practical intellect to judge how to use what it knows. By knowledge we understand how created things and human realities contribute to our relationship with God, and we can judge how to use them. Knowledge gives us a grasp of the practical value of things in terms of our growth in grace. The connection of knowledge with the Sacrament of Reconciliation is obvious.

Wisdom is the gift of *appreciating* what we see. By wisdom we have an insight into the beauty and goodness, into the value of God's truth and of God himself. Wisdom is essentially an enlightened taste for God and the things of God. Nothing helps us to grow in appreciation for God so much as experiencing the sweetness of union with Jesus Christ. In Communion we have this experience. *Eucharist*, therefore, is the sacrament we associate with wisdom.

Wisdom also helps us appreciate human and created values, but it does this by helping us see them in relationship to God. Wisdom helps us to view and appreciate all things as coming from God and as leading us to God. It has been called the virtue (or habit) of seeing all things in the light of our last end, which is union with God forever. Here we have a point of contrast between wisdom and knowledge. Knowledge helps us to appreciate the practical values of created things in our spiritual lives. Wisdom helps us to appreciate the value of God in himself and as our final destiny.

Both gifts lead to an enhanced appreciation both of God and of the world; but their direction is different. Whereas by knowledge we rise from appreciation of creatures to appreciation for God, by wisdom we move in the other direction: from appreciation for God to appreciation of creatures. By the Gift of Wisdom we appreciate all things more because we see them in the light of, and through the appreciation we have for, God.

St. Ignatius of Loyola is inviting us to experience the Gift of Wisdom when he tells us in *The Spiritual Exercises* to contemplate how all blessings and gifts "descend from above" as rays of light descend from the sun, or waters flow from a fountain.

The other gifts help us to act

The other three Gifts of the Holy Spirit: Piety, Fortitude and Fear of the Lord, are gifts which help us to *act*, to carry out into action what we *see* by understanding and wisdom and are able to *judge* effectively by wisdom and knowledge.

Fear of the Lord strengthens the will against the allurement of lesser goods by giving us an affective appreciation of God as our only true security and good. This gift (called in Scripture "the beginning of wisdom") helps us to put God first in our lives and to dedicate ourselves entirely to His service. Because of this we can associate it with the sacrament of adult commitment to God, which is *Confirmation*.

Piety is the gift of "family love." It helps us to give to every person the loyalty and love appropriate to the relationship we have with him or her. Through Piety we relate to God as Father and to all the other members of the human race as being (or as called to be) our brothers and sisters in Christ. Through piety the whole Church relates to Jesus Christ as Spouse. This gift is appropriately associated with *Matrimony*.

Fortitude is the gift which strengthens our wills to undertake what is difficult or dangerous. As such it is particularly necessary for those engaged in the apostolate of transforming the world. This gift is rooted in Christ's victory over sin and death on the cross. We associate it with the Sacrament of Anointing.

Taken together, then, the Gifts of the Holy Spirit enable our intellects and our wills to "interface" with the Holy Spirit so that we might *see, judge* and *act* on the level of God.

The Fruit of Love

The Sacrament of Eucharist increases wisdom within us by letting us literally "taste and see that the Lord is sweet." That is why the "Fruit of the Spirit" appropriate to this sacrament is *Love*. We love what we long for; we long for what we love. The more we experience and appreciate what Jesus really is for us, the more we love and long for Him.

It is my unprovable but firm belief that all Catholics have mystical experiences during Communion. On those occasions when we are able to enter into ourselves in silence and be conscious of what we are experiencing at Communion time, is it not true that we "know we know" that Jesus is within us?

This knowledge is not the same as mere information. We know there is a man in the White House and an American flag on the moon; that is information. When we receive Communion, however, what we know is that Jesus is present within us. This is more than information; this is experience. I think it is a mystical experience. It is a faint foretaste, a dim preview, of the happiness of heaven. It is an experience of being united to God, of possessing and enjoying Him in love.

The Communion Service: celebration of heaven

Here we have the essential reason why Communion (and the

whole Communion Service portion of the Mass) has an "eschatological" focus: it is because Communion is an eschatological experience, an experience of the blessings that are to come.

This is also the reason why Communion strengthens us and motivates us for the *apostolate*. If we "taste and see" how good the Lord is, then we will be motivated to bring the whole world into union with Him. This means to "bring all things in heaven and on earth into one under Christ's headship" (see Ephesians 1:9-10). The Eucharist motivates and strengthens us to give ourselves to this task as faithful *stewards* of the Kingship of Christ.

The Eucharist is the sacrament of love. It calls us, quite simply, to convert to loving the Lord our God as He loves us. His love is total gift of himself to us, expressed in the Eucharist. Our love is total gift to Him in return.

This is what the Eucharist calls us to.

CHAPTER 13

Am I Working
For the Kingdom of God?

*Being loyal to Jesus
as a friend*

Friends help each other. What am I doing in my life to help Jesus Christ? The driving desire of Jesus' life was — and is — to establish the Kingdom of God. This means to bring every human life and activity under the life-giving direction of God's truth, God's power, God's love. In the measure that any human person, any family, any business, any social event or political project is surrendered to the rule of Jesus Christ, in that same measure the Kingdom is being realized on earth. And Christ needs us to make it happen.

Jesus didn't come to take the place of human activity on earth. He came to renew human nature, not to retire it. When Jesus died on the cross His work was finished and just begun: He had redeemed the world and launched it. New life was poured out on earth. But this new life needed to grow and spread and begin to transform human society through the activity of those who would accept it. What was "finished" on the cross was only the beginning of the transformation of the world.

The friends of Jesus are those who work to realize the desires of His heart. This means to bring about the transformation of society throughout the world.

The leaven must work in the world

The world is not transformed in church. When I ask groups, "How many of you are actively involved in the apostolic work of your parish?" I always get the same response. All the people who raise their hands are eucharistic ministers, CCD teachers, members of the parish council, money-raisers for the bazaar.

People who are "just" mothers and fathers never raise their hands. Nor do the people who are working so hard at their jobs that they never have time to attend a meeting at church, much less participate in a project.

You would think that raising children at home was not an apostolic work of the Church! In reality, it is the most important contribution anyone can make to the realization of the Kingdom of God. This is the first and most important apostolic work of any parish.

After raising the children, the next most important apostolic work of any parish, or of the Church as a whole, perhaps, is the incarnation of the Gospel in life through the things people do at home and on their jobs. The Good News is best put into practice not in church, but at home and on the job where people really live. Everything else done in the parish is to prepare people for this. This is where the Good News meets the world and transforms it. The bread only rises where the leaven meets the dough.

Apostolate: life or project?

For some reason people tend to write off the time they spend on their jobs as time lost to the apostolate. Working hours are hours not available for more meaningful service. Catholics think of "apostolic work" as something people do in their spare time, on the side. Only priests and nuns — and some rare Church-employed laity — work "full time" in the "apostolate." Everyone else is a part-time volunteer.

For the laity we speak of apostolic "projects." For the clergy it is a life. That is why we feel that the priests and nuns and brothers are closer friends of Jesus than the laity are. The clergy and Religious seem more dedicated to His interests. They work full time for the Kingdom of God, while the laity just work for a living and volunteer for "apostolic" work in their free time.

This way of looking at things may be true. It may be that in fact lay Catholics are not working full time — at home, at work and at play — for the Kingdom. If this is the reality of the situation, it shouldn't be. There is no such thing as a Christian who is not called to work full time for the Kingdom of God. This is what Jesus tells us we should be working for — not just to make a living.

The one thing Jesus tells us *not* to work for, in fact, is a living! He is explicit about that: "Do not worry about your livelihood," He says, "Your heavenly Father knows all that you need. Seek first His kingship over you, His way of holiness, and all these things will be given you besides" (see Matthew 6:25-34).

The only valid, lasting reason a Christian has for working at all is to contribute to the establishment of God's Kingdom on earth — to help "bring all things in the heavens and on earth into one under Christ's headship" (see Ephesians 1:10). This is what the lay, the secular, vocation of Christians is: to transform the world. The only way Christ's Kingdom will be established on earth is through lay Christians bringing under His reign the reality of this world: the reality of family and social life, of business policies and political options.

The laity's field of action

The world is not transformed in church. The world is transformed only on its own turf, in the midst of its own life and activity. This means family life, social life, student or professional life, and civic life. This is where the laity are. It is their natural — and their vocational — milieu.

Vatican II defined lay Christians — "secular" Christians — as people who "live in the world, that is, in each and in all of the secular professions and occupations." The laity live "in the ordinary circumstances of family and social life, from which the very web of their existence is woven."

This is what gives the laity their special place, their special character, their unique and exclusive advantage in establishing the Kingdom of God. They are a part of the action of this world. They are there where it happens. They are able to transform it from within.

The clergy and Religious make great contributions from the sidelines: They coach; they exhort; they watch trends; they sound warnings; they teach principles, guidelines and skills. They train the laity to know Jesus Christ, to read Scripture, to pray, to listen to the Holy Spirit, to discern, to

109

make Christian decisions. By their own example of renunciation they lessen the laity's fear of losing the things of this world. They encourage them to take risks.

But they don't set foot on the field. The clergy and Religious are not involved — at least, not as the laity are — in family and social life, in business and politics. They have taken their stakes out of the pot and, for the most part, have renounced their share of the winnings in this world. For that reason they are not in the game like the laity are. They do not have the same stake in its outcome. Nor can they change its direction from within. In family and social life; in business and politics, they are not the real players. The laity are. That is why Jesus Christ depends on the laity to change the direction of life in this world; to transform the structures of society, renew family and social life, bring Christianity into business and politics. This is what it means to be called to lay life in the Church: it is a vocation, not just to take a part, but to *be* a part of the secular life of this world; to establish the Kingdom of God on earth by being an active element in society and letting Jesus Christ reign in and through everything one does.

The real apostolate of the laity is to transform the things they are already doing — full time. The apostolate of the laity is not to talk to fellow workers about Jesus on coffee breaks! It is to speak to the world through the work they do; through the work itself. The real apostolate of the laity is to let the ideas and values, the principles and vision of Jesus Christ transform their professional activity. The laity fulfill their apostolate in and through the work they do eight to ten hours a day. Anybody who does this will have a chance of being heard if he speaks about the Gospel on a coffee break. But just as what he does during the coffee break is not his real job, so the words he speaks then are not his real apostolate. His "word" spoken in the world is the word of his life's work itself.

The corruption of our environment does not come from what people say or do not say to one another on coffee breaks. It comes from the business decisions which give us pornography in the shopping centers, inferior products in the marketplace, environmental hazards in industry, violence on the international scene, inflation, recession and unemployment. It comes from bad choices, selfish behavior, shortsighted policy decisions on the part of individual human beings in management and labor, in schools and offices and government. Most of what is wrong in our world is due to individual, personal failures to follow right values in family and social life, business and civic activity. It is mainstream involvement which takes the world off course, and only mainstream involvement will redirect it.

That is the lay apostolate. It is also what it means to be a steward of the Kingship of Christ.

Fidelity to Jesus the Lord

Friendship for Jesus Christ means having His interests at heart always in everything one does. It means being a *faithful steward* in family and social life, in professional and political involvement. It means being a friend who is conscious at every moment that the one thing Jesus most desires is to bring every area of human life and activity under His life-giving reign. It means believing in Him as Lord, supporting Him in His mission, and bringing His Kingdom to be.

Friends help each other. How am I helping — in my family and social life, business and civic performance — to bring all things into harmonious unity under the headship of Jesus Christ? The way I answer this question will be a measure of my *stewardship*, my fidelity as friend to Jesus, King and Lord.